RELIGION AND CULTURE

RELIGION AND CULTURE

Gifford Lectures

Delivered in the University of Edinburgh
in the year 1947

BY

CHRISTOPHER DAWSON

NEW YORK
SHEED & WARD
1948

PRINTED IN U. S. A.
BY POLYGRAPHIC CO. OF AMERICA

291.17
D27

Baker + Taylor

2 45

21 Jan 71

Contents

CHAPTER		PAGE
I.	NATURAL THEOLOGY AND THE SCIENTIFIC STUDY OF RELIGION	3
II.	THE ELEMENTS OF RELIGION: GOD AND THE SUPERNATURAL	25
III.	THE RELATION BETWEEN RELIGION AND CULTURE	47
IV.	THE SOURCES OF RELIGIOUS KNOWLEDGE AND THE RELIGIOUS ORGANS OF SOCIETY . .	65
	(I) Prophets and Divination	
V.	THE SOURCES OF RELIGIOUS KNOWLEDGE AND THE RELIGIOUS ORGANS OF SOCIETY . .	87
	(II) Priesthood and Sacrifice	
VI.	THE SOURCES OF RELIGIOUS KNOWLEDGE AND THE RELIGIOUS ORGANS OF SOCIETY . .	109
	(III) Kingship	
VII.	THE DIVINE ORDER AND THE ORDER OF NATURE. SACRED SCIENCE	131
VIII.	THE DIVINE ORDER AND THE SOCIAL ORDER. SACRED LAW	153
IX.	THE DIVINE ORDER AND THE SPIRITUAL LIFE. THE WAY OF PERFECTION . . .	175
X.	RELIGION AND CULTURAL CHANGE . .	197

37958

CHAPTER I

Natural Theology and the Scientific Study of Religion

THE RELATION between Natural Theology and humanist culture. Its development as the classical theology of humanism and its failure to withstand the radical secularization of the humanist tradition. The new attitude to religion which characterizes the reaction against the Enlightenment. The romantic philosophies of religion and the study of symbol and myth. The concept of evolutionary development and the comparative study of religions. Influence of anthropology and psychology on religious studies. Development of the comparative science of religion during the last sixty years. The necessity of maintaining a theological foundation.

Natural Theology and the Scientific Study of Religion

I

(i)

THE TERMS of the Gifford foundation presuppose the existence of a science of Natural Theology which is competent to study the nature of the Divine Being and the relations of man and the universe to Him—the greatest of all possible sciences, but nevertheless a strictly natural science and one which is of the highest importance to human culture.

This is a tremendous claim and one which would be denied to-day by most modern philosophers and many modern theologians. The historian, however, cannot fail to recognize what a great tradition this claim has behind it—a tradition which is closely related to the main stream of Western thought. For Natural Theology is the theology that was natural to Humanism, and its rise and decline follow that of the humanist culture itself. From the Renaissance to the eighteenth century and even later the development of Natural Theology went hand in hand with that of Humanism. And if to-day Natural Theology is hard-pressed by the convergent attacks of Dialectical Theology and Dialectical Materialism, humanist culture has also lost its prestige and the whole structure of the rational cosmos of Western man has been shaken to its foundations.

The humanist culture was essentially the culture of an intellectual élite. It was never a complete self-sufficient organism like the great religious cultures of earlier times. It was rather an artificial structure superimposed on the existing body of Christian society. Yet in spite of this artificial secondary character, it was an active and creative power which made its influence felt in every aspect of Western life. In fact, during the centuries when Western Christendom was so profoundly divided by controversy and sectarianism, by religious wars and religious persecutions, it was Humanism which was the chief unifying element in European culture, since it provided the only ground on which the members of the different nations and the different churches could meet on equal terms. In other words a common education and a common literary culture took the place of a common faith and a *communio sacrorum* as the chief remaining bond of European unity.

But although Humanism was thus closely associated with the secularization of European culture, it was by no means altogether irreligious. In this respect I think the Humanists have been ill served by their modern apologists and admirers, with the result that the current popular conception of the Renaissance and the humanist culture is erroneous and one-sided. It is not in Poggio or Machiavelli or Vanini[1] that we find the typical representatives of the humanist attitude to religion, but in Erasmus and More and the Christian Platonists. The new appreciation of the good of nature and the dignity of man and the rational optimism of the humanist ethos demanded a

[1] Poggio Bracciolini, 1380–1459. Papal secretary and chancellor of the Republic of Florence.
Niccolo Machiavelli, 1469–1527. Secretary and diplomatic agent of the Republic of Florence.
Lucilio Vanini, 1585–1619. Neapolitan priest and freethinker; travelled throughout Europe, imprisoned in London and finally executed as an atheist at Toulouse.

4

natural theology to justify them. The humanists saw the world as a rational order which could be explained only as the work of divine Reason, as a work of divine art which shows forth the mind of the divine Artist.

This humanist view was summed up by Campanella[1] in the famous sonnet in which he speaks of the visible world of nature as the book in which God has revealed His power, His wisdom and His goodness. It is man's vocation to be the interpreter of this divine hieroglyphic, since by reason and by his spiritual nature he has an innate kinship with the divine author.

> *Il mondo è il libro dove il Senno eterno*
> *scrisse i propri concetti, e vivo tempio*
> *dove, pingendo i gesti e'l proprio esempio,*
> * di statue vive ornò l'imo e'l superno;*
> *perch'ogni spirto qui l'arte e'l governo*
> * leggere e contemplar, per non farsi empio,*
> * debba, e dir possa: Io l'universo adempio,*
> *Dio contemplando a tutte cose interno.*
> * Ma noi, strette alme a'libri e tempii morti,*
> *copiati dal vivo con più errori,*
> *gli anteponghiamo a magistero tale.*
> * O pene, del fallir fatene accorti,*
> *liti, ignoranze, fatiche e dolori:*
> *deh torniamo, per Dio, all'originale!*

" The world is the book where the eternal Wisdom wrote its own concepts, and the living temple where, depicting its

---

[1] Tommaso Campanella, O.P. (1568–1639), philosopher, poet, friar and conspirator: one of the most original figures of the late Renaissance. He spent thirty years of his life in prison, mostly in Sant' Elmo at Naples, where all his greatest poetry was written, as well as his Communist Utopia *The City of the Sun* which is his best known work. He died at Paris under the protection of Richelieu.

deeds and own example, it adorned the depth and the height with statues;

" that every spirit here, lest it become impious, may learn and contemplate art and law, and can say: I fulfil the universe, by contemplating God within all things.

" But we, souls fettered to books and dead temples, copied from the truth with many errors, place them above such teaching.

" O suffering, discord, ignorance, labour, grief, make us aware of our mistake. Ah, by God, let us return to the original."[1]

This, I take it, is the classical experience of the humanist Natural Theology which was already proclaimed in the book of Raymond Sebunde,[2] was fully developed in the following centuries by the Christian Platonists and the humanist theologians and philosophers from Marsilio Ficino to Yves de Paris and the Cambridge Platonists, and still lived on in a somewhat impoverished and arid form in the Natural Religion of the Enlightenment, the apologetic Natural Theology of Paley and the Bridgewater Treatises.

There was nothing new or of startling originality in this doctrine: it consisted to a great extent of the commonplaces of the doctrine of the schools and the Fathers and the philosophers of antiquity. It was by definition a rudimentary theology or as Bacon put it, " that knowledge or rudiment of knowledge concerning God which may be obtained by the light of nature and the contemplation of his creatures." The difference lay not in the novelty of the doctrine, but in the new value that was attached to it and the new importance it assumed in a society that no longer possessed religious unity.

[1] *Poesie*, ed. Gentile, p. 16. Translation by E. G. Gardner.
[2] Raymond Sebunde or Sibiuda, a follower of Raymond Lull and probably a Catalan, died at the University of Toulouse in 1436. He is remembered chiefly on account of Montaigne, who translated his book into French at his father's behest and later wrote the famous *Apology of Raymond Sebunde* which is the longest of his Essays.

In the ages of faith, Natural Theology had no separate existence. It was a part of the common Christian theology and had no independent significance except to professional theologians. But in the age of religious division when Europe was rent asunder by rival theological systems, Natural Theology acquired a new value as the one certain and universal foundation of religious truth in a world where everything was disputed. It was for this reason no doubt that the humanist Pierre Bunel recommended Raymond Sebunde's *Natural Theology* or *Book of Creatures* to Montaigne's father as a work most profitable and fitting to times when the unquestioned reign of a universal authority had been broken and the most sacred articles of faith had become the subject of popular debate.

It is perhaps as difficult for the present generation to understand the attraction of this simple theology of reason as it is for us to understand the revolutionary appeal of the idea of the Law of Nature which was developed during the same period from the same premises. Nevertheless it is impossible to ignore their historic importance or their influence on the development of modern thought. For the men of the New Learning could no more dispense with the idea of God than the men of the Old Learning. The more completely the new philosophy and the new science realized their ideal of a rational universe, the more they needed the idea of God as the source and principle of intelligibility. As Descartes wrote, " the certitude and truth of all science depend on knowledge of God and on that alone " for " the certitude of all other truths is so dependent on this one that without the knowledge of God it would be impossible ever to know anything else."

(ii)

This conception of God as the sole principle of intelligibility is characteristic of the new philosophy no less in its orthodox Christian representatives like Malebranche and Berkeley than in the totalitarian Natural Theology of a Spinoza. But in so far as it made God not only the author of Nature but the medium of our understanding and the guarantee of our empirical knowledge, it profoundly changed the traditional character of Natural Theology and exposed it to a two-fold attack: first of all from devout Christians like Pascal who felt that this god of mathematical truth was a God of the Epicureans and not the God of the Christians " who fills the soul and heart of those whom he possesses "; and secondly from the sceptics who realized that the Cartesian divorce of matter and spirit was a two-edged weapon which could be used to undermine and destroy the whole intellectual edifice which had been constructed so laboriously by the age-long efforts of Christian philosophers and theologians.

In this double offensive the Christian critics of Descartes played into the hands of their opponents, who were indebted to them not for their arguments but for the technique of their offensive. For it became a commonplace with the enemies of religion to cover their main attack on the credibility of Theism by an insincere tribute to " the truths of our most holy religion ". " A person seasoned with a just sense of the imperfections of our natural reason," writes David Hume, " will fly to revealed truth with the greatest avidity while the haughty dogmatist persuaded that he can erect a complete system of theology by the mere help of philosophy, disdains any further aid and rejects this adventitious instructor. To be a philosophical sceptic is, in a man of letters, the first and most essential step towards being a sound believing Christian."[1]

At first sight it seems anomalous and paradoxical that the humanist Natural Theology should have received its most dangerous criticisms not from the theological reactionaries

[1] *Dialogues Concerning Natural Religion*, XII *ad fin.*

but from men like Bayle and Hume and Voltaire who were themselves nominally Deists. For when the cause of Humanism seemed at last triumphant and the whole culture of the age was dominated by the spirit of rational optimism, which had its metaphysical roots in the Cartesian Natural Theology, the foundations of the ideological structure were undermined by the leaders of the Enlightenment themselves.

The causes of this breakdown were religious rather than philosophical. The humanist Natural Theology had flourished as long as it was in contact with the living tradition of Christian culture. But as soon as Deism broke the vital contact and attempted to make Natural Theology the autonomous principle of a purely rational religion, it was powerless to withstand the disintegrating criticisms of the sceptics. From the beginning Deism had no religious life of its own. It was created artificially to serve the controversial purposes of the Enlightenment, and when these aims were secured, it was discarded by its creators.

It is true that at a relatively late stage in its history, it received a temporary infusion of life from the influence of Rousseau. But Rousseau's appeal to the irrational forces of sentiment and emotion was a dubious boon. For it not only taught philosophers like Kant to value the spiritual intuitions of the Common Man above the metaphysical proofs of the Natural Theologians, it also taught the Common Man to regard his emotional convictions as infallible truths. However lukewarm and superficial was the natural religion of the Enlightenment, it was at least sincere in its devotion to the virtue of tolerance. But in its new form the later Deism became an intolerant and sanguinary cult. It was in the name of the religion of natural virtue that Robespierre destroyed his enemies, and the Festival of the Supreme Being, of June 1794, when the new religion was solemnly inaugurated, marked at the same time the climax of the Terror.

II

These catastrophic years saw a profound change in the current of European thought. They saw the end of the Enlightenment and the passing of the aristocratic society which had produced the humanist culture. The political revolution coincided in time with a spiritual and emotional revolt against the rationalism of the Enlightenment and the whole tradition of eighteenth century culture. The century which had begun with the religious rationalism of Locke and Christian Wolff ended with the apocalyptic irrationalism of Blake's prophetic books. And in these shapeless outpourings of religious genius, it is Natural Religion and the God of Natural Religion which are the great objects of Blake's denunciations. " Man must and will have some religion," he writes, " if he has not the religion of Jesus, he will have the religion of Satan, and will erect the synagogue of Satan, calling the Prince of this World ' God ', and destroying all who do not worship Satan under the name of God. . . . Deism is the worship of the God of this World by the means of what you call Natural Religion and Natural Philosophy, and of Natural Morality or Self-Righteousness, the selfish virtues of the Natural Heart. This was the religion of the Pharisees who murdered Jesus. Deism is the same, and ends in the same."

But the Spectre, like a hoar-frost and a Mildew, rose over Albion,
Saying: ' I am God, O Sons of Men! I am your Rational Power!
Am I not Bacon and Newton and Locke, who teach Humility to
    Man,
Who teach Doubt and Experiment? and my two Wings, Voltaire,
    Rousseau?

Where is that Friend of Sinners, that Rebel against my Laws,
Who teaches Belief to the Nations and an unknown Eternal Life?
Come hither into the desert and turn these stones to bread!
Vain, foolish Man! wilt thou believe without Experiment,
And build a World of Phantasy upon my Great Abyss,
A World of Shapes in craving lust and devouring appetite? '[1]

This revolt against the Natural Theology of the Enlightenment
which finds its purest and most direct expression in Blake's
prophetic utterances, pervades the thought of the age and
appears in a more rationalized and diluted form in the system-
building of the idealist philosophers and the apologetics of
the romantic theologians.

Everywhere we find, on the one hand, a new appreciation
of the positive religious values revealed in history and in the
religious experience of the individual, and on the other an
attitude of criticism and often of contempt towards the traditional doctrine of the rational demonstrability of the existence
of God. Religion is feeling and imagination: not reasoning
and demonstration. And the more immediate and incommunicable the feeling, the higher the religion. No doubt there
was no lack of reasoning about religion, but it was a reasoning
that was more akin to that of the Gnostics and the theosophists
than to that of the Natural Theologians. In spite of the honour
that was paid to Spinoza by Schelling and his contemporaries,
it was not Spinoza but Boehme the mystical theosophist who
had the deepest influence on the philosophical theism of that age.[2]

This influence of Boehme was not simply due to the attraction

---

[1] *Jerusalem*, f. 52 and f. 54, lines 15–24.
[2] Jacob Boehme, shoemaker and mystic (1575–1624), had little influence
on German thought until the end of the eighteenth century when his works
suddenly acquired an extraordinary vogue among the romantics, especially
the poet Tieck and Baader the philosopher. In this country, on the other
hand, his influence was strongest during a much earlier period. His
works were translated during the Civil Wars by John Sparrow and others

that any kind of speculative mysticism had for the romantics. It was much more specific than that. Boehme himself was a Natural Theologian, of a sort—at least, he would certainly have claimed that title. But he stands at the opposite pole from the Natural Theology of the Enlightenment, and this most of all at the point on which the romantic idealists attacked their eighteenth century predecessors most sharply. For it was not merely the rationalism of the Enlightenment that disgusted the new age. It was above all its optimism: that naïve and insensitive optimism which declares with Pope that " Whatever is, is right " and justifies the ways of God to Man in the style of Bernardin de St. Pierre who demonstrated that God made fleas black so that it should be easier for us to catch them, and had divided melons into sections, so that it would be easier to cut them up in equal portions for the sake of domestic harmony.[1] Against all this childishness the new generation insisted on the reality of the problem of evil and the tragic sense of life, which was not accidental or avoidable, but rooted in the very nature of things. And they found in Boehme a natural theologian who was so far from ignoring these things that he brought them back to their roots in Eternity, so that the " bitterness " which is at the root of nature has its ground in the Dark Side of the Divine Nature itself.

It is remarkable that the same line of thought is to be found in a more orthodox form in the work of the great Catholic writer of an older generation who was the most implacable enemy of the Enlightenment and the intellectual leader of the

and may have had some influence on the early Quakers. Later, he was studied by Sir Isaac Newton, William Law was his disciple, and the sect of the Behmenists flourished again in the early eighteenth century.

[1] Compare especially his *Harmonies de la Nature* (1814), the reductio ad a bsurdum of Deist optimism. As Joubert wrote, when it was first published: " Ses Harmonies nous font aimer les dissonances qu'il bannissait du monde, et qu'on y retrouve à chaque pas."

religious reaction. Joseph de Maistre[1] was not a philosopher but a man of the world—a most unworldly man of the world it is true, a diplomat who was more concerned with the divine meaning of history than with his career or his political future. No one was more determined than de Maistre to justify the ways of God to man, but in order to do so he reversed the traditional theology of the Enlightenment and based his apologetic on that dark side of reality to which his predecessors had closed their eyes. To him the abyss of human suffering and crime was a more effective witness to the existence and majesty of God than all the facile arguments of current apologetics. His philosophy of history was not the theory of human progress and enlightenment but the revelation of divine justice and divine judgment. He humbled man in the dust of history in order to exalt the majesty of God.

III

This reaction against the Enlightenment led de Maistre to view with greater sympathy all those elements in ancient and oriental religion which had hitherto been regarded by philosophers and historians as irrational and barbarous. Sacrifice, Karma, asceticism, tabu, all became comprehensible and religiously valid in de Maistre's philosophy of history. It is significant that in the *Evenings at St. Petersburg* the discussion centres on a long quotation from the Laws of Manu which cannot have been very familiar reading to the literary public of that date, and throughout the dialogues he calls in the wisdom of the East to answer the reasoning of the West.

---

[1] Joseph de Maistre (1753–1821), the contemporary of Talleyrand, was the most austere and uncompromising adversary of the Enlightenment and the principles of the Revolution. His most active years were spent in Russia as the penniless minister of the exiled King of Sardinia, but he had a European influence as the intellectual leader of the Catholic revival in the early nineteenth century.

This, of course, was not completely new. It was, I think, the first time that the new knowledge had been used for theological purposes, but ever since 1808 when Friedrich von Schlegel published his book *On the Language and Wisdom of the Indians* the new world of oriental religion had been opened to the West.

During the early part of the nineteenth century the study of religion was transformed by the flood of new knowledge which came pouring into Europe from the East, from India and Persia, from Egypt and Babylonia, from China and the Far East as well as from Central America and Polynesia. The abstract *a priori* constructions of eighteenth-century rationalism faded before the rich and complex realities of man's actual religious experience. The discovery reinforced the conviction of the idealist philosophers that history was itself the key to spiritual reality, so that for them the only true Natural Theology was the philosophy of history. The great task of the philosopher was to construct an intelligible synthesis in which the successive spiritual achievements of the great world epochs and world religions were shown as stages in the progressive self-revelation of the Absolute Spirit.

In this way the traditional distinction of Natural Theology and revelation is entirely abolished, since nature is revelation, and revelation is the hermeneutic principle of the science of religion in general. The mythology and religious symbolism of oriental and primitive peoples were interpreted as the hieroglyphic record of this universal revelation, and the science of comparative mythology developed by F. Creuzer and F. C. Baur, by Schlegel and Schelling, enjoyed for a short time an extraordinary popularity and influence.

It was from this school,[1] for all its lack of intrinsic scientific

[1] The following are the most important works of this school:
F. Creuzer: *Symbolik und Mythologie der Alten Völker, Besonders der*

value, that the new science of comparative religion had its origin. For it led men to pay attention to the more obscure and non-rational aspects of religion which the theologians of the Enlightenment had despised and neglected. Above all it emphasized the unity of human religious development, so that mythology and ritual, folk-lore and saga, theology and mysticism were all treated as parts of a living whole, a tree rooted in the earth of history and geography, and sending its topmost branches into the clouds of mysticism and theological speculation. The ambitious claims of this new science or pseudo-science were very soon dismissed by the criticisms of scholars like Lobeck (1781–1860) and Otfried Muller (1797–1840), but the ideal of an all-inclusive science of religion remained in the background and was revived in a positivist and evolutionary spirit by the new " Science of Comparative Religion " which acquired academic status in the second half of the nineteenth century.

The great popularizer of the new science in this country, F. Max Müller, was himself the heir of the earlier romantic movement, the son of a romantic poet and the disciple of Schelling and Bopp.[1] In fact Max Müller's science of Comparative Religion was hardly less speculative than Baur's science

---

Griechen, 4 in-8°, Leipzig, 1810–12; 2nd. edit., 6 vols. ibid., 1819–23.
J. J. von Goerres: *Mythengeschichte der Asiat. Welt.* 2 in-8°, Heidelberg, 1810.
F. C. Baur: *Symbolik und Mythologie, oder die Naturreligion des Alterthums.* 2 vols. in 3 in-8°, Stuttgart, 1824–25.
P. E. von Lasaulx (1805–61).
Neuer Versuch einer alten auf die Wahrheit der Thatsachen Gegründeten Philosophie der Gesch., 1856.
Ueber die Theolog. Grundlage alter philos. Systeme. 1856.
Die Prophetische Kraft der Menschlichen Seele in Dichtern und Denkern, 1858.

[1] Franz Bopp (1791–1867), the founder of Comparative Philology, was himself the disciple of the Romantics and it was F. Schlegel who first conceived the idea, and even coined the name, of the new science which Bopp afterwards developed.

of Comparative Mythology. But the intervening period had seen an enormous accession of knowledge, not only in the case of oriental and archaeological studies, but also in the understanding of the religion and culture of the primitive peoples where vast new fields of study were being gradually opened to scientific research.

The publication of J. B. Tylor's *Primitive Culture* in 1871, which was the first important synthesis of the new anthropological knowledge, marks an epoch in this field. It was translated into Russian in the following year, into German in 1873 and into French in 1876–8.

At the same time the secularization of the theological faculties led to the establishment of chairs of the History of Religion and of the Comparative Study of Religion in the Dutch and French Universities. By the close of the century the new science of Comparative Religion or the natural history of religion had everywhere taken the place of the old Natural Theology as the only recognized scientific approach to religious problems.

The Gifford Lectures are, I believe, the only foundation of that period of which the aims are still defined in the traditional terms of Natural Theology. And even here Campbell Fraser, who was essentially a man of the old tradition, records in his autobiography that he was at first unwilling to undertake the lectures because he supposed that they were concerned with the historical science of religions more than with the philosophy of Theism.

And it is true that from the first the relations of the science of religions to philosophy were by no means clear. The new science developed in an age of positivism and agnosticism. It aimed at the study of the facts of man's religious development, while abstaining from theological and philosophical judgments. This attitude was determined, on the one hand, by an ideal of scientific objectivity borrowed from the physical sciences and, on the other, by the practical necessity of establishing a neutral territory on which orientalists, missionaries, anthropologists and psychologists could co-operate harmoniously.

Actually, however, this programme of philosophic neutrality proved to be impracticable. Both the comparative method and the concept of evolutionary development involved judgments of value which had philosophical implications. The numerous works on the history of religion during the later nineteenth and early twentieth centuries depend for the most part, consciously or unconsciously, on the older philosophical syntheses of Hegel and Comte; and even to-day it is still necessary to insist on the intimate relation that exists between the naturalistic theories of evolutionary development current since the nineteenth century, and the strictly idealist conception of an inevitable progress to perfection which is a manifestation of the progressive self-realization of the absolute spirit in history.

In one form or another—from the Christian idealists on the Right to the dialectical materialists on the Left, these ideals dominated the development of the new science of religion, and where they were absent it tended to disintegrate into a formless collection of unrelated specialisms.

It is true that the wealth of material accumulated by these specialisms provided an ample field for study, but this science no longer possessed any criterion by which to judge the intrinsic value and significance of the religious phenomenon. In place of the objective science of the Existence and Nature of God, which had been the ideal of the old Natural Theology, it could attempt only an extensive survey of the forms of human behaviour as conditioned by non-rational beliefs. But the new science suffered from the same fundamental weakness as the old Natural Theology. Both of them were equally rationalistic and reduced the deepest problems of human consciousness to superficialities. The Natural Theology of the Enlightenment reduced the Living God of Christian tradition to the celestial engineer of the cosmic mechanism, while the science of comparative religion created a museum of dead cults and anthropological curiosities.

This was the situation as William James saw it when he delivered his famous lectures at Edinburgh nearly fifty years ago. He sought a solution to the dilemma in a new existential study of religious phenomena in their experimental actuality. And though he did not find a genuine solution, he at least revealed the fundamental defect of the older methods. He saw that " the recesses of feeling, the darker, blinder strata of character are the only places in the world in which we catch real fact in the making." " It is where the further limits of our being plunge into an altogether other dimension of existence from the sensible and merely understandable world " that religion has its origin, and the spiritual forces that originate in this region have a real and transforming effect on human life and social culture.

In this way William James turned the attention of both the psychologists and the philosophers to a deeper kind of experience than either the old Natural Theology or the earlier phases of the science of religion had envisaged. And since his day the psychologists have increasingly devoted themselves to the study of the Unconscious and demonstrated the immense importance of the unconscious mental processes for human thought and behaviour.

This new psychological approach has had a profound influence on the study of religion. It has meant that those very elements in religion which were ignored or explained away by the earlier philosophic and rationalist students of religion have now been put in the forefront of scientific study. And we have already come to understand much more about these unknown territories of the soul which have been of such importance for religious experience and religious action—the world of symbol and myth, of vision and prophetic utterance—as well as the unconscious forces of sublimation and repression that condition the moral aspects of the personality.

No doubt psychology has provided new and easily manipulated weapons for the rationalist who sees religion as the result of a delusional process of projection which can be liquidated by scientific methods of analysis. But this is not the only or the most normal conclusion of the psychological approach. The deeper men look into the hidden life of the psyche, the more disposed will they be to recognize the reality and creativity of the spiritual forces which manifest themselves in the religious experience of the human race.

That was the conclusion of William James and it is emphasized even more strongly by contemporary psychologists like C. G. Jung who regard the traditional archetypes of religious symbolism as the master keys to unlock the deepest levels of spiritual reality. For, he writes, " myths are first and foremost psychic manifestations that represent the nature of the psyche ".[1] And " whatever is true of this primitive lore is even more unconditionally true of the ruling world religions. They contain what was originally the hidden knowledge of revelation and set forth the secrets of the psyche in glorious images. . . . Indeed we are forced to say that the more beautiful, the more grandiose, the more comprehensive is the image that has come into being and been handed on, so much the farther is it removed from our experience."[2]

All this has a striking resemblance to the theories of the

[1] " Archetypes of the Collective Unconscious " in the *Integration of the Personality*, p. 54.
[2] *Ibid.*, p. 56.

early nineteenth century symbolists, like Creuzer and Baur, who believed that religious myths and symbols are not arbitrary imaginative phantasies but eternal images of psychic reality which have the same relation to the conscious activity of rational thought as the life of the race has to that of the individual.

Now these images and the religious experience out of which they arise are, as William James used to insist, absolutely authoritative and invulnerable in their own field, but equally they are unauthoritative and incommunicable to the reason on the plane of rational science and philosophy and natural theology. On the one side we have a world which is full of religious richness and depth but incapable of rational demonstration. On the other, an intelligible order without spiritual depth or direct contact with religious truth. No doubt it is possible, as history has shown, to construct proofs of religion and of the existence of God which are valid even within this rational order. But the life of these constructions is derived from the other order. In themselves they are essentially arid and if one may use the word, heartless, so that the religious man who is confronted with them will always reply with Pascal " Not the god of the philosophers and the scientists, but the God of Abraham and Isaac and Jacob—*Deum meum et Deum vestrum* ".

The problem of religious thinkers throughout the ages has been to build a bridge between these two worlds. Traditionally the bridge was built by authority—the collective social guarantee of a supernatural revelation—and this solution still retains and must ever retain its validity so long as the historic world religions remain. But this is not the case with the solutions which were constructed from the rational rather than from the religious side, like the Natural Theology of the Enlightenment, or the more ambitious philosophies of religion created by the romantics and the idealists.

For to-day the two worlds have fallen further apart than ever before. The world of reason has become more arid and spiritually void, and the world of the soul has lost the consecrated ways by which it expresses itself in the world of culture and has been left at the mercy of the forces of darkness which are the negative and destructive aspects of the Unconscious.

This disintegration of modern civilization between a science without significance and the spirit which can only express itself in self-destruction has come so near to us in these last years that no thoughtful man can consider it with equanimity. And it is no longer the fate of a particular culture that is in question, but the doom of the human race.

Nevertheless had we but time to think,—if we are granted a reprieve from the enormous perils we have incurred so thoughtlessly—there is no necessary reason why the dualism of which I have spoken should not eventually be overcome.

The very fact that modern psychology has concentrated its attention on the Unconscious and has realized its scientific importance shows that the two worlds are not completely impenetrable. And in the same way the soul seeks understanding and revolts against the claims of reason only when reason refuses to understand and rejects the reality of the soul's deepest experience and the sources of its spiritual life. In the higher cultures the existence of religion has always involved the existence of theology—that is to say, a rational system of religious knowledge. All the higher religions do in fact assert the existence of a science of divine truth and base their teaching upon it. And it is obvious that if there is no true knowledge of the object of religious experience, religion loses its validity, and even its social coherence, and becomes an irrational impulse like any other delusional form of psychosis.

In fact, however, the divorce between the psyche and the reason which this alternative supposes is abnormal, unnatural and morbid, since it is only by a conciliation and co-operation of the two that the world of culture in which we live and in which man has always lived has come into existence. And this task of conciliation—this building of a bridge between the two worlds—has been the historic function of religion. To use a different metaphor—the world religions have been the key-stones of the world cultures, so that when they are removed the arch falls and the building is destroyed.

It is the business of the historical science of religion to show how religion has fulfilled this task: how the vital relation has been maintained between the depths of the Unconscious and the surface of the social order: how religion asserts its internal spiritual autonomy and how it is moulded and conditioned by the influences of environment and social function.

It is only when all this has been understood that it is possible to deal with the fundamental problems of Natural Theology: the transcendent element in religious experience and the eternal absolute validity of religious truth. Yet, as I will endeavour to show in the following lecture, it is necessary to make a provisional acceptance of these principles in order to understand religion at all.

For the study of religion begins and ends on the theological level, and not on the level of sociology and history, indispensable as these are for the understanding of religion in culture and in human life.

The Elements of Religion: God and the Supernatural

THE TRADITIONAL teaching of Natural Theology on man's natural knowledge of God. Religion founded on the worship of superhuman powers and the consciousness of transcendent being. (1) The Hellenic and humanist proof of divinity from the order of the universe. The external world as a manifestation of divine power. The sense of cosmic transcendence. (2) The proof of divinity from spiritual experience. The sense of spiritual transcendence characteristic of the deeper forms of religious consciousness. The identification of the object of this transcendent spiritual intuition with the transcendent cosmic power, characteristic of the higher religions. Monotheistic tendency of this sense of spiritual transcendence. The sense of Transcendence in primitive religion. Magic and Religion. The concept of the Sacred and the Numinous. Shamanism and the emphasis on visionary experience. Psychological continuity between primitive and advanced types of religion. The concept of revelation.

The Elements of Religion: God and the Supernatural

I

I HAVE suggested that a new historical approach to the study of religion is essential alike for the student of Natural Theology and for the student of human culture. But if we adopt this approach, we must be on our guard against certain dangers that have always affected the comparative study of religion from its beginnings in the eighteenth century down to our own days. Historians have always tended to ignore the theologians, and sociologists to level down religion to its sociological and cultural elements. But no study of religion can be fruitful unless it accepts the reality and the autonomy of religious knowledge. Any so-called science of comparative religion which treats its subject in terms of psychopathology or economic determinism is sterile and pseudo-scientific.

What then is the specific nature of the religious phenomenon? All religion is based on the recognition of a superhuman Reality of which man is somehow conscious and towards which he must in some way orientate his life. The existence of the tremendous transcendent reality that we name GOD is the foundation of all religion in all ages and among all peoples.

As Calvin writes at the beginning of the *Institutes:*

Quemdam inesse humanae menti, et quidem naturali instinctu, divinitatis sensum, extra controversiam ponimus : siquidem nequis ad ignorantiæ praetextum confuguret, quandam sui numinis

25

intelligentiam universis Deus ipse indidit, cujus memoriam assidue renovans novas subinde guttas instillat: ut quum ad unum omnes intelligant Deum esse, et suum esse opificem, suo ipsorum testimonio damnentur, quod non et illum coluerint, et ejus voluntati vitam suam consecrarint. Sane sicubi Dei ignorantia quaeretur, nusquam majus extare posse ejus exemplum verisimile est, quam inter obtusiores populos et ab humanitatis cultu remotiores. Atqui nulla est etiam, ut Ethnicus ille ait, tam barbara natio, nulla gens tam efferata, cui non insideat haec persuasio, Deum esse. Et, qui in aliis vitae partibus minimum vîdentur a belluis differre, quoddam perpetuo religionis semen retinent, adeo penitus omnium animos occupavit, adeo tenaciter omnium visceribus inhaeret communis illa praesumptio. Nulla ergo quum ab initio mundi regio, nulla urbs, nulla denique domus fuerit quae religione carere posset; in eo tacita quaedam confessio est inscriptum omnium cordibus divinitatis sensum.[1]

I quote the testimony of Calvin rather than that of St. Thomas or St. Augustine because it is with the former that we find the traditional Christian doctrine of Natural Theology reduced to a minimum. No theologian has taken a more gloomy view of the

---

[1] *Institutio Christianae Religionis*, Lib. I, cap. 3.

" We lay it down as a position not to be controverted, that the human mind, even by natural instinct, possesses some sense of a Deity. For that no man might shelter himself under the pretext of ignorance, God hath given to all some apprehension of his existence, the memory of which he frequently and insensibly renews; so that as men universally know that there is a God, and that he is their Maker, they must be condemned by their own testimony, for not having worshipped him and consecrated their lives to his service. If we seek for ignorance of a Deity, it is nowhere more likely to be found, than among tribes the most stupid and farthest from civilization. But, as (the celebrated) Cicero observes, there is no nation so barbarous, no race so savage, as not to be firmly persuaded of the being of a God. Even those who in other respects appear to differ but little from brutes, always retain some sense of religion, so fully are the minds of men possessed with this common principle, which is closely interwoven with their original composition. Now since there has never been a country or family, from the beginning of the world, totally destitute of religion, it is a tacit confession, that some sense of the Divinity is inscribed on every heart."

ruinous or impotent state of human nature abandoned to itself, none has been less inclined to set a value on any knowledge which man can acquire concerning the nature of God by the power of his own reason. Yet even for Calvin there is no question of the fact that the human mind possesses a natural knowledge of the existence of God which is inseparable from its very constitution—" *doctrina quae non in scholis primum discenda sit sed cujus quisque ab utero magister est et cujus neminem oblivisci natura ipsa patitur quamvis hoc multi nervos omnes intendant* ". " A doctrine which has not to be learnt in schools, but of which every man is master from birth and which nature herself allows no man to forget although many strive with all their might to do so."

In fact, whenever there is any recognition of any kind of religious truth, some place, however lowly, must always be found for Natural Theology. Its radical denial is only possible where religion is regarded as a form of mass delusion which may have had a great importance for human culture, but can have no objective truth or validity.

This view, which is so widespread in modern times, is historically associated with humanist rationalism and with modern man's growing confidence in his own power and his own knowledge. During the last century or two the world of culture has grown until it has subjugated the world of nature and pushed back the frontiers of the superhuman spiritual world beyond the boundaries of consciousness. And since man had become all in all, it was natural to believe that religion also was a purely human phenomenon that belonged to the world of man and had no relation with any external reality. In the days of his ignorance man created religion as an instrument to overcome the perils and to satisfy the needs of his life, in the same way as in the days of his enlightenment he had created science. The gods were the images of his hopes and fears; the creatures of his imagination, the servants and instruments of his will to power.

There is something plausible and rationally attractive about this theory. For the religion that we find as a historical reality in primitive culture is not the natural religion of the philosophers—not " religion within the limits of pure reason "—it is religion within the limits of human nature—man-made religion. And when man makes his religion he makes it not with his reason alone, but much more with his hopes and fears. The weaker man is, and the lower his stage of culture, the greater is his dependence on the mysterious powers that rule the world. The darkness presses close on the little space that is illuminated by the fitful light of human reason and controlled by the uncertain power of human will and design, and man's hopes and fears populate the surrounding darkness with all kinds of divine and supernatural powers whose hostility must be warded off and whose favour and help must be gained, in order that he may survive.

Nevertheless primitive man in his weakness and ignorance is nearer to the basic realities of human existence than the self-satisfied rationalist who is confident that he has mastered the secrets of the universe. The latter has focused all his attention and all his activity on the region which can be explored by human reason and controlled by human will, and has thereby made it wider and more habitable, but he has not changed the fact of its ultimate limitation. In so far as he is content to live within this world of his own creation—the artificially lit and hygienically conditioned City of Man—he is living precariously on a relatively superficial level of existence and consciousness, and the higher he builds his tower of civilization the more top-heavy it becomes. For his nature remains essentially the same as that of primitive man—the nature of a rational animal, limited internally by the conditions of his consciousness and externally by his dependence on non-human forces which transcend his animal existence.

II

No doubt it is an amazing miracle that man should have been able to overcome the animal conditions of his existence so far as to build the towering edifice of civilization and to construct the rational order of scientific knowledge. But however high he builds and however far his scientific vision and invention reach, there always remain further regions—perhaps infinite regions—of being beyond his grasp and out of his sight.

Thus the range of man's rational activity is bounded on the one hand by the depth of his unconscious mind and on the other by the transcendent element in external reality. And this element of transcendence is a primordial element of human experience. Man is born into a world that he has not made, that he cannot understand and on which his existence is dependent. In actual fact, social authority and the world of culture take hold of him from the cradle and thrust back the frontier of transcendence behind the authority and omniscience of parents and schoolmasters. It is only in the poetic imagination which is akin to that of the child and the mystic that we can still feel the pure sense of mystery and transcendence which is man's natural element.

Where this element survives intact we have no need to look further to find a natural basis for religion. There is a famous passage that has been preserved by Cicero from Aristotle's lost dialogue *On Philosophy* which puts this in a vivid and picturesque form. " Imagine," he says, " a race of underground men living a civilized existence, provided with every necessity and luxury, but deprived of the light of day. And if one day the jaws of the earth were opened, and they beheld for the first time the earth and the seas and the shining sun and the changing moon and the unchanging order of the heavens, such men would surely confess that the gods exist and that these things are the works of god."

This Aristotelian parable is equally appropriate to the case I have in mind of the man who emerges from the man-made, artificially conditioned world of culture and faces the reality of an external world or order of being which transcends the farthest range of his power and knowledge. And in fact it has always been the traditional argument of Natural Theology that man has only to look out and to look up in order to see the manifest proofs of Divine power and wisdom.

This is the oldest and the most universal of the formal proofs of the Divine existence, since it appealed equally to the Hebrew poet and the Greek philosopher, to the Christian theologian and to the Renaissance scientist. But in modern times its appeal has been weakened if not destroyed, by the mechanization of nature which was the work of Cartesian and Newtonian physics. As William James said, " the days are over when it could be said that for science herself the heavens declare the glory of God and the firmament showeth His handiwork. Our solar system with its harmonies is seen now as but one passing case of a certain sort of moving equilibrium in the heavens, realized by a local accident in an appalling wilderness of worlds where no life can exist. In a space of time which as a cosmic interval will count but as an hour it will have ceased to be."[1]

Nevertheless this dwarfing of the scale of man's world ought to increase rather than diminish man's sense of transcendence and of the fragility of the rational world that he has constructed. If the Hellenic ideal of a visible intelligible divine order has disappeared, the argument of Job which appeals to the overwhelming reality of the mystery of transcendence has acquired new force. This is not an argument that satisfies

[1] W. James, *Varieties of Religious Experience*, p. 491.

man's natural desire for reassurance and security, which has often been regarded as the source of religious belief: it is emphatically not an instance of that " delusional transformation of reality " which Freud regards as the essence of religion. Yet there can be no question of its religious power or of the fact that it appeals equally strongly to the most primitive and to the most sophisticated minds.

It does not, however, make the same appeal to the average man who lives contentedly within the world that he has made for himself. And it is precisely here that the weakening or disappearance of the old argument from design has involved a loss of the intellectual foundation of religious belief which was formerly accepted as a necessary, universal and unquestionable truth.

III

But if the modern world has lost the old naïve extraverted belief in a rational universe which clearly manifests the power and intelligence of its Divine Author, the other way of spiritual experience is still open. Natural Theology says not only look up and look out—it also says look down and look in, and you will find the proofs of the reality of God in the depth of your own nature. The philosopher and the scientist may question the probative force of this experience. They may say that any feelings we may have beyond bodily processes are but our experience of our own conscious processes, or if, as more commonly, they admit the reality and the importance of a psychological region below the surface of consciousness, they may say that this is nothing but the irrational substratum of man's animal nature. But the men of religious experience—the saints and the sages— have always taught that the further man penetrates into the depth of his consciousness and of what lies below his consciousness, the nearer he approaches to spiritual reality.

31

And there is no doubt that we have here—in the experience of transcendence which is associated with the movement of introversion—one of the ultimate and absolute sources of historic religion in all ages and cultures. I do not think that sufficient weight has been given to this experience in the traditional proofs of Theism, no doubt because the natural theologians have felt that any experience of this kind goes beyond the limits of rational knowledge and demonstration to which they have confined themselves. Nevertheless, as William James remarks, the mere existence of such experiences breaks down the exclusive claim of the rational consciousness to represent the totality of possible modes of knowledge. And he himself went considerably further than this since he argued that even when we exclude what he calls the " over-beliefs " and confine ourselves to the residual elements, we are left with " the fact that the conscious person is continuous with a wider self through which saving experiences come, a positive content of religious experience which it seems to me is literally and objectively true, as far as it goes."[1]

But if we admit the existence of such intuitions as a fact of religious experience, we are bound, it seems to me, to go further and take account of their significance to the religious man who has in some sense assimilated them and related them to his way of life and his conception of reality.

And here we have an immense body of testimony from East and West—from all the great traditions of the world religions which unite in asserting the presence of God in the depths of the soul as its eternal transcendent " ground ".

Here, for example, is a typical passage from one of our mediaeval Western mystics, the Blessed John Ruysbroeck (1293-1381):

" In the most noble part of the soul, the domain of our

[1] W. James., *op. cit.*, p. 515.

spiritual powers, we are constituted in the form of a living and eternal mirror of God; we bear in it the imprint of his eternal image and no other image can enter there." " This image is found essentially and personally in all men; each man possesses it whole and entire and all men together possess no more of it than does each one. In this way we are all one, united in our eternal image which is the image of God, and the source in us all of our life and our coming into existence. Our created essence and our life are joined to it immediately as to their eternal cause. Yet our created being does not become God any more than the image of God becomes a creature."[1]

This is a classical religious interpretation of the basis of religious experience, and it is obvious that we cannot exclude it *a priori* since it is an essential part of the phenomenon that we are discussing.

Religion does not arise from the experience of men like Archdeacon Paley, but from that of men like Ruysbroeck, and the thought of Ruysbroeck is more genuinely Natural Theology than the thought of Paley, even though it may be less communicable and less adapted to logical discussion.

For religion has its origin in the depths of the soul and it can be understood only by those who are prepared to take the plunge. It may be as Jacobi said a *salto mortale*, but it is not, as he supposed, a leap from knowledge to faith.[2] That is the basic fallacy of the Natural Theology of the Enlightenment. The difference between the discursive reason and the intuition of the contemplative is not the same as the difference between the natural and the supernatural (in the technical, theological

---

[1] Ruysbroeck. *The Mirror of Eternal Salvation*, ch. VIII.

[2] F. H. Jacobi (1743–1819), like Al Ghazali, criticized the philosophers for maintaining that logical demonstration is superior in value and certainty to intuitive perception. He taught that philosophy is a kind of logical criticism which can define and explain but cannot reach beyond itself. All our knowledge of Reality, whether material or spiritual, is derived from immediate perception, and this is a kind of miracle which we must accept by an act of faith—a leap in the dark from which there is no escape.

sense of the words)—between reason and faith; it is simply a question of the different levels of consciousness which are equally parts of human nature. And the identification of human nature with its extraverted rational aspects confuses and prejudices the whole approach to the study of religion.

IV

The possibility of Natural Theology and indeed of any genuine theology depends on our view of the nature of these deeper levels of consciousness. If they are merely forms of sub-rational experience, then the essential phenomena of religion can be studied only psychologically or pragmatically, and no philosophical conclusions can be drawn from them. But if they represent a real form of knowledge, then they are susceptible of scientific treatment and there is room for a science of religious truth such as theology.

It is, however, a well-known fact that many philosophers in all ages have asserted not only that a real knowledge is possible on this deeper level of consciousness but that this is the highest and most genuine form of knowledge accessible to man. There is a remarkable consensus on this point among all the traditional philosophies of the Eastern World, alike in India and China and Central and Western Asia. In India especially the whole philosophical tradition which represents a very considerable contribution to human thought centres upon this question of the existence of a transcendent intuition, and the relation of this deeper knowledge to the other forms of experience.

Modern Western philosophy will, no doubt, explain this as a typical example of that snobbish exaltation of the art of knowing by the leisure class at the expense of the useful and laborious activities of the worker which Professor Dewey described in the first of his Gifford Lectures. And it must be admitted that it is easy to construct a sociological rationalization of the Vedanta in terms of the caste system.

But this explanation is far too superficial to explain so general and so profound a tendency of human thought. The movement of introversion, by which man attains a consciousness deeper than that of his discursive reason but no less real, appears to be a universal human experience, common to almost all forms and stages of human culture. As the Vedantists say, in speaking of *Vidya*, it does not rest on philosophy since it is an independent direct intuition which is not affected by the limitations of philosophy and has not to answer philosophical difficulties.[1]

No doubt they would go further and assert that what is known is the absolute self-existent Being—Brahman without second; but this belongs to the secondary stage of philosophical interpretation. What is given in the experience itself is the existence of transcendent spiritual Being in and beyond the depths of the soul itself. This simple intuition of transcendent spiritual Being is latent in many forms of religious experience where it is not overtly recognized. It is in fact an ultimate natural basis of the idea of God and the condition of man's higher religious development.

There is, of course, the other way of religious experience of which I have already spoken—the sense of cosmic transcendence which finds its classical religious and literary expression in the Book of Job. And it is difficult to over-estimate the importance of this, especially for primitive religion. But it is only when the two ways of religious experience are brought together and the transcendent power behind the world is related to the transcendent spirit beyond the soul, that the former realizes its full religious significance. When the *mysterium*

---

[1] cf. G. Dandoy, *An Essay on the Doctrine of the Unreality of the World in the Advaita*, p. 53 (Calcutta, 1919). This remarkable essay has been re-published in 1932 in a French translation by L. M. Gauthier, edited by Jacques Maritain (*Questions Disputées*, vol. V) under the title *L'Ontologie du Vedanta*.

tremendum which is manifested in the universe is worshipped for itself, we have the typical religious developments of paganism and the worship of the powers of nature. But when the God of Nature, the transcendent power which creates and governs the world is identified with the God of the Soul, the transcendent spiritual Being, the presence of which is obscurely felt in the profoundest states of human consciousness, then the basis exists for a higher type of development, such as we find in the historic world religions.

The classical instance of this is to be found in Indian religion and philosophy, where the identification of Atman—the transcendent Self—with Brahman—the transcendent cosmic power—is formulated with exceptional clarity and where it becomes the foundation of the whole religious and philosophical development of orthodox Hinduism. And alike in India, and in the tradition of Greek thought as represented by the Neo-platonic synthesis, it was the intuition of spiritual Being which was the source of the monotheistic element which imposes itself incongruously but irresistibly on the heterogeneous polytheism of their inherited religious traditions.

For the experience of cosmic transcendence tends to be multiform and leads naturally to a pluralist or polytheist theology, whereas the intuition of transcendent spiritual Being always tends to unity, to such a degree, indeed, that it has often produced a denial of the possibility of anything except the One existing.

Western philosophy started with the Hellenic conception of Nature. Its *raison d'être* was to explain and rationalize nature, and God was ultimately brought in as the key-stone of the philosophic edifice—as the First Cause or the Prime Mover. Eastern philosophy, on the other hand, started with the principle of Transcendent Being and then attempted to explain the world, or the existence of relative conditional

existences, in terms of the absolute. As Père Dandoy puts it,
" we say: perish the rest, but the reality of the world must
stand. The Vedantist says: perish the rest, but the Supreme—
Parabrahma—must remain what it is, the eternal self-sufficing
unconnected fulness of Being."[1]

But whichever path is followed, Natural Theology involves
the affirmation of transcendent Being: whether this is attained
by a cosmological enquiry which leads to the Eternal Cause
and First Principle of Nature, or whether it is reached by a
direct intuition of the Absolute as present in us and transcending
the deepest limit of our consciousness.

V

Obviously this whole notion of Transcendence to which
we are continually brought back is not merely a colourless
negative like Herbert Spencer's Unknowable. It is a negative
which is highly charged with spiritual energy and represents
the ultimate and irreducible element in religious experience. No doubt it is true that in a thoroughly secularized
and rationalized culture, men can recognize the limits of
their external knowledge and their internal consciousness,
without thereby making any affirmation of a religious nature.
For they will see the whole universe of nature and mind
as entirely destitute of anything that is qualitatively different
from the fraction of it that has been fenced in and tilled by
human culture. In all the infinite expanses of time and space,
there is no spiritual principle except the human mind, and no
transcendent order except the order of culture. But this
conception of an infinite universe which nevertheless is her-
metically sealed against the intrusion of any higher order of
reality is an extremely rare phenomenon in human thought. Its
most striking expressions both in antiquity and in modern

[1] Dandoy., *op. cit.*, p. 3.

times are reactions against an established and privileged religious tradition and are often animated by a sort of religious conviction, as we see in the case of Lucretius who writes of his atomic universe with the fierce enthusiasm of a Hebrew prophet denouncing idolatry.

The religious attitude towards transcendence, on the other hand, appears to be far more deeply rooted in human nature and far more widely present in human culture. It is closely bound up with that sense of the Holy or the Numinous of which Rudolf Otto has written and which he regards as a purely *a priori* category which " issues from the deepest foundation of cognitive apprehension which the soul possesses " and has " its independent roots in the hidden depths of the spirit ".

The study of primitive religion during the last century has tended to emphasize more and more the importance of primitive ideas of supernatural power which are not necessarily derived from a belief in particular gods or spirits or from the technique of the professional magician. Words like the Polynesian *Mana*, the North American *Orenda*, *Wakan*, *Manito*, *Yok* are found amongst very many primitive people and denote an impersonal power—" an ocean of supernatural energy " as J. R. Swanton calls it—which manifests itself in nature and in visions and in all events which appear portentous or miraculous. The anthropologists may describe this element as " magical ", the students of comparative religion as " numinous " or " dynamistic " and the theologians as " divine ", but whatever term is used the distinctive thing about it is its transcendent character. It is always felt as something outside man's common experience: an *other* world, an *other* power, an *other* being, which forcibly or mysteriously imposes itself on this world of human beings and human power as greater or more powerful or more sacred. No doubt in many cases this transcendent quality is attached to persons and things,

38

as in the case of Mana which is associated with the person of the sacred chief in Polynesia, or as with the West African fetish and the North American " medicine bundle ". But this does not detract from its transcendent character, any more than the power of working miracles or the veneration of sacred relics conflicts with the doctrine of divine transcendence in the higher religions. In fact, the conception of Mana can be most easily understood as a pagan analogy to the Christian conception of grace.

The universality and importance of this sense of transcendence in the most primitive forms of religion can hardly be questioned, since they have left their mark in the history of human speech. It is true, as I have already observed, that in primitive religion it is the sense of external cosmic transcendence which predominates. Nevertheless this cannot be entirely detached from the internal intuition of transcendence even though the latter is obscure, confused and rudimentary.

Thus in the primitive culture to which I have referred, the greatest importance is always attached to the supernormal psychic experiences of dream and vision, trance and ecstasy, and the men who possess such experiences are the religious leaders and the intellectual teachers of the community. No doubt it seems absurd to compare the primitive Shaman or the witch doctor with the mystic or the Vedantist philosopher who claims to have attained a pure intuition of absolute transcendent being. Nevertheless, however crude is the expression of primitive religious experience and however much it is contaminated with the practise of magic and conjuring, we cannot exclude the existence of a residual element of genuine religious experience. For in the majority of cases, it is the aim of the diviner and the Shaman to transcend the limits of ordinary knowledge and to attain that deeper level of consciousness which we have described already as the natural basis of religious experience. No doubt it is much harder to distinguish

39

the quality and value of such experience in primitive religion, but even in the higher religions we are faced with a similar difficulty. Among the Yogis and Sanyasis of India, or the dervishes of Islam, for example, we find instances of every type and level of religious experience from the highest trancendent intuition to the crudest forms of thaumaturgy.

In none of these cases is it possible to explain the higher elements by the lower or the lower by the higher. If William James is right in his conclusion " that there is in the human consciousness a sense of reality, a feeling of objective presence, a perception of what we may call ' something there ', more deep and more general than any of the special and particular senses, by which the current psychology supposes existent realities to be originally revealed",[1] then one must expect this intuition to be found in the most diverse conditions of human thought and culture without any necessary relation to the capacity for rational expression.

In the case of primitive culture the diviner or seer possesses none of the armament of philosophical thought and theological tradition with which the higher religions and cultures are provided. Here accordingly we must expect to find an apparently arbitrary combination of profound individual experience with irrational symbolism and crude material forms. The primitive has the same ultimate experience of reality on the deeper level of consciousness as the civilized man, but he has no criterion to separate what is spiritually transcendent from what is naturally extraordinary. He cannot connect his intuition of transcendent power with any rational metaphysical system; but he can superimpose upon it some image or intuition of external reality which makes a powerful psychological appeal to him, since primitive thought develops by association and images rather than by arguments and ideas. Hence his vision of the external world is related to religion and to the world

[1] James., *op. cit.*, p. 38.

40

of the gods in an entirely different way to that of civilized man. To the primitive hunter, for example, the beasts are not merely a source of food supply, and an occasional danger, they are mysterious beings which are in a sense superior to man and nearer to the divine world. The strength of the bull, the swiftness of the deer, the flight of the eagle, the cunning of the serpent, are revelations of superhuman, and consequently divine, power and glory. And the same is true of the attitude of the primitive farmer to the earth and the fruits of the earth. However low is the level of his culture, man cannot but recognize the existence of laws and rhythms and cycles of change in the life of nature in which his own life is involved. There is day and night, summer and winter, birth and death; the rain falls and the grass grows, the seed ripens; but these things are not mechanical changes or "natural" material facts, they are divine mysteries to be adored with trembling. Behind these appearances there are divine powers—gods or spirits or undifferentiated magical forces which must be propitiated and served if man is to live.

But the obscurity and apparent illogicality of primitive thought do not destroy its religious importance. On the contrary, it is inevitable that in proportion as primitive religion is deep and rich, the more obscure and symbolic will be the form of its expression. There is every reason to believe that religion held just as large a place in primitive life and culture as in that of any historical civilization. The difference between the religious and the irreligious is not a difference between levels of culture but the difference between levels of consciousness. And we can see from history and experience that this difference of psychological levels has no necessary relation to the social condition of a people or to the intellectual culture of the individual. However far back we go in the history of the race, we can never find a time or place where man was not conscious of the soul and of a divine power on which his life depended.

VI

It is of course true that this primordial knowledge of God and the soul is very remote from anything that can be called Natural Theology. Primitive man is not concerned with abstract truth but with the reality and power of the forces on which his life depends, and his religion finds expression in myths and rites or sacred techniques. It is only at a later stage of culture, when social organization is sufficiently advanced to leave room for learning and study, that we can expect to find any systematic tradition of rational thought. Nevertheless, as we shall see in the course of these lectures, it is precisely in the sphere of religion that this advance was first achieved and that the idea of systematic scientific knowledge first arose. In the religious literature of India we can trace the whole process by which there was developed first a highly specialized class devoted to the study of the sacred formulas and ritual techniques and secondly a movement of theological thought and speculation concerning ultimate religious truths which finally became concentrated on the primary intuition of the absoluteness of the Being which underlies and transcends alike the Self and the cosmic process.

When this point is reached we can indeed speak of Natural Theology but in spite of its genuinely philosophical character, and its reliance on direct spiritual intuition, the Vedanta itself claims the authority of revelation in the strict sense of the word. " The authority of the Veda," writes Sankara,[1] " with regard to the matter stated by it is independent and direct just as the light of the sun is the direct means of our knowledge of form and colour; the authoritativeness of human dicta, on the other hand, is of an altogether different kind, as it depends on an extraneous basis and is mediated by a chain of teachers and

[1] *Vedanta Sutras*, trans. G. Thibaut. *Sacred Books of the East*, vol. XXXIV, p. 295.

tradition ".[1] Nay more, the truth of the supreme intuition is itself established by the authority of Scripture and not vice versa.[2]

This holds good of all the historic religions: everywhere revelation is regarded as the primary source of religious truth, and intuition and reason are secondary. And this is true in the sense that positive, historic religion is always primary, and philosophical or theological religion is the result of a secondary reflective activity. The concept of revelation is as old as religion itself, since the most primitive types of religion always rely on the authority of an immemorial tradition and/or on some supernatural means of communication with the higher powers such as omens, divination and the visions and inspired utterances of Shamans or prophets. The continuity between the primitive tradition of divination and shamanism and the higher developments of philosophic thought is to be seen even in Greek philosophy with Empedocles and the Pythagoreans—not to mention the daemon of Socrates—and in the Eastern religions the connection is still closer and more unmistakable.

Of course I do not mean that the concept of revelation is confined to the lower forms of culture and the more primitive types of religion. On the contrary it is universal and found in different forms at every stage of religious development, whereas the idea of Natural Theology is found in only a few cultures and there only at a relatively advanced stage of development. Every school of Natural Theology is preceded by a revealed theology and in most cases proceeds from it. Thus the Hellenic

[1] Sankara (c. A.D. 788–850) taught the strict monist (Advaita) interpretation of the Vedanta and is usually regarded as the greatest philosopher of Hinduism. His influence has been maintained by his order—the Dasnamis—and the superior of his monastery at Sringeri in Mysore is the religious head of orthodox Brahminism. The members of his order have to lay aside the sacred thread and give up sacrifices, since he taught that the Way of Knowledge is the only way of release.

[2] ibid., p. 101.

43

Natural Theology was preceded by the Orphic revelation, the Vedantic Philosophy develops directly from the revealed teachings of the Upanishads, as its name—*Uttara Mimamsa,* the Later Enquiry—denotes, and the humanist Natural Theology is a rational superstructure erected on the foundations of the Christian theology of revelation. Any scientific study of religion in its historic manifestations and in its relations with human culture must therefore take account of the different revelations and of the religious traditions which arise therefrom. But in so far as it attempts not merely to record the history but to understand the nature of religion, it is bound to refer and defer to Natural Theology, since the latter is nothing more or less than the philosophic or scientific study of religious truth.

If religious truth is entirely outside the range of rational enquiry, then there is no room for Natural Theology, but at the same time the historical science of religion also loses its value and becomes no more than an exploration of a series of spiritual culs-de-sac, the study of certain forms of irrational thought and behaviour. Therefore although we cannot regard Natural Theology as a complete self-sufficient body of religious truth, as it was to the philosophers of the Enlightenment, it must always retain its importance as the indispensable link between theology and philosophy and between the world of historic religion and the domain of rational thought. For as I pointed out in the previous chapter, the breach of communion between the spiritual and the rational order is the most formidable problem that confronts the modern world, and though this problem cannot be solved by Natural Theology, the recognition of the function of Natural Theology is one of the necessary conditions for its solution; since the rejection of Natural Theology means that God and the soul, the primary realities of the spiritual world, are rejected as dead words that have no significance and value for the mind of man.

44

CHAPTER III

The Relation between Religion and Culture

CULTURE as an organized way of life, based on a common tradition, and conditioned by a common environment. Specialization of cultural traditions. Every culture represents a spiritual community and involves common beliefs and common ways of thought. Consequent mutual interpenetration of culture and religion. The cultural function of religion is both conservative and dynamic: it consecrates the tradition of a culture and it also provides the common aim which unifies the different social elements in a culture. The cultures of the past have never been conceived as purely man-made orders. They are founded on a religious law of life which co-ordinates the life of society with the life of nature and with the divine powers which rule the life of nature and the life of man. Thus the relation between Religion and Culture is always a two-sided one. The way of life influences the approach to religion, and the religious attitude influences the way of life. We may explain any given religion as the product of a process of social conditioning, but we cannot exclude the opposite alternative —the moulding and transformation of the social way of life by religious forces. Revolutionary influence of religion on culture and history as seen in the case of Islam, etc.

The Relation between Religion and Culture

THERE is still a certain amount of distrust of the sociological concept of culture among historians and men of letters, owing to the feeling that it is an alien importation into our language. Since the days when Tylor wrote his book on Primitive Culture, however, it has been adopted so widely by anthropologists and ethnologists, that it seems pedantic to object to a word which has acquired a scientific status as a specific term for which there is no satisfactory alternative.

A social culture is an organized way of life which is based on a common tradition and conditioned by a common environment. It is therefore not identical with the concept of civilization which involves a high degree of conscious rationalization nor with society itself, since a culture normally includes a number of independent social units.

The fact that a culture is a way of life adapted to a particular environment involves a certain degree of social specialization and the canalization of social energies along certain lines. We see this most clearly in the case of isolated marginal cultures, like that of the Esquimaux in the Arctic or that of the Bushmen in South Africa. In these cases the inter-relation of social organism, economic function and geographical environment is so complete that culture becomes inseparable from race.

But this does not mean, as the racialists believe, that culture is the result of predetermined racial inheritance. On the contrary it would be more true to say that race is the product

47

of culture, and that the differentiation of racial types represents the culmination of an age-long process of cultural
segregation and specialization at a very primitive level, just
as in modern times nationality and the differentiation of
national types is the result of the growth of special cultural
traditions rather than vice versa.

It is indeed remarkable how rapidly the human type is
modified or transformed by a new way of life or a new environment. Take a few hundred thousand nineteenth century
English and Irish, transplant them to Australia and let them
adapt their social habits and organization to this new environment, and in a century you find a new human type which is both
physically and psychologically different from that of the parent
society.

Nevertheless in spite of these far-reaching changes, the
factor of cultural tradition remains predominant. The new
Australian type is not a variety of the native Australian type
but of the British type, so that to an Australian aboriginal the
two will probably appear so similar as to be indistinguishable.
For the way of life of any particular society exerts so powerful an
influence on its individual members that hereditary differences
of character and predisposition are worked into the pattern of
culture as the multi-coloured threads are woven into the design
of a fabric. Thus culture is the form of society. The society
without culture is a formless society—a crowd or a collection of
individuals brought together by the needs of the moment—
while the stronger a culture is, the more completely does it
inform and transform the diverse human material of which it
is composed.

What then is the relation of culture to religion? It is clear
that a common way of life involves a common view of life,
common standards of behaviour and common standards of
value, and consequently a culture is a spiritual community

48

which owes its unity to common beliefs and common ways of thought far more than to any uniformity of physical type. Now it is easy for a modern man living in a highly secularized society to conceive this common view of life as a purely secular thing which has no necessary connection with religious beliefs. But in the past, it was not so. From the beginning man has already regarded his life and the life of society as intimately dependent on forces that lie outside his own control—on superhuman powers which rule both the world and the life of man. "No man," said an Indian hunter, "can succeed in life alone, and he cannot get the help he needs from men."

This conviction that "the way of man is not in himself", that it is not for man to walk and direct his own steps, is as old as humanity itself. We can find most clear and moving expressions of this belief among the primitive peoples—most of all perhaps among the hunting peoples like the North American Indians whose conception of dependence on spiritual powers has been described with exceptional fullness by a series of excellent scholars and observers, like I. O. Dorsey, F. Boas and Ruth Benedict.

But it is also found amongst much more primitive races, and needless to say in all the higher religions.

Therefore from the beginning the social way of life which is culture has been deliberately ordered and directed in accordance with the higher laws of life which are religion. As the powers of heaven rule the seasons, so the divine powers rule the life of man and society, and for a community to conduct its affairs without reference to these powers, seems as irrational as for a community to cultivate the earth without paying any attention to the course of the seasons. The complete secularization of social life is a relatively modern and anomalous phenomenon. Throughout the greater part of mankind's history, in all ages and states of society, religion has been the great central unifying force in culture. It has been the guardian of tradition, the preserver of the moral law, the educator and the teacher of wisdom.

And in addition to this conservative function, religion has also had a creative, conative, dynamic function, as energizer and life giver. Religion holds society in its fixed culture pattern, as in Plato's Laws, or as in the hierarchic order of Sumerian and Egyptian culture; but it also leads the people through the wilderness and brings them back from captivity and inspires them with the hope of future deliverance.

Religion is the key of history. We cannot understand the inner form of a society unless we understand its religion. We cannot understand its cultural achievements unless we understand the religious beliefs that lie behind them. In all ages the first creative works of a culture are due to a religious inspiration and dedicated to a religious end. The temples of the gods are the most enduring works of man. Religion stands at the threshold of all the great literatures of the world. Philosophy is its offspring and is a child which constantly returns to its parent.

And the same is true of social institutions. Kingship and law are religious institutions and even to-day they have not entirely divested themselves of their numinous character, as we can see in the English coronation rite and in the formulas of our law courts.

All the institutions of family and marriage and kinship have a religious background and have been maintained and are still maintained by formidable religious sanctions. The earliest social differentiation and the one that has had the most potent influence on culture has been due to the development of specialized social classes and institutions, charged with the function of maintaining relations between society and the divine powers. The fact that this class has almost invariably been responsible in whole or in part for the education of the community and the preservation of sacred tradition and learning gives it an exceptional importance in the history of culture; and we must study the specific form it takes in any particular culture or religion before we can begin to understand it. The Sumerian and Egyptian temple priesthoods, the Brahmin caste in ancient India, the clergy and the monaslic orders in mediaeval Christendom are not merely religious institutions, they are also vital social organs in their respective cultures. And the same is true of the Shamans, the medicine men and witch doctors among primitive peoples although our current terminology often blurs the distinction between the sorcerer, whose function is non-social or anti-social, and the priest, who is the recognized religious organ of the community —a confusion which has been increased by the attempt to draw a rigid and exclusive line of division between religion and magic.

The more primitive a culture is, of course, the less room there is for an explicit differentiation of social functions, but on the other hand, the more directly is its religion bound up with the elementary needs of life, so that the social and economic way of life is more clearly interpenetrated by and fused with religion than is the case in the higher cultures.

Thus among the Australians there was no true priesthood and the leadership in religion as in other matters fell to the old men who were the natural leaders of the tribe and the guardians of tradition. Nevertheless they possessed a most elaborate and highly organized system of religious rites to ensure the continuity of the life of the tribe and the maintenance of its food supply—a regular liturgy, which in some instances, as described by Spencer and Gillen, occupied the community almost continuously for three or four months at a time. In this case the way of life of the community is conceived as dependent on another and a sacred world—the world of the divine totemic ancestors—from which the spirit comes and to which it returns, and the totemic ceremonies provide the way of access and communion between the life of the tribe and the other world of the sacred *alcheringa* age.

It is difficult for a civilized man to understand either the religious significance or the cultural importance of such ceremonies. But to the primitive the dance or mime is at once the highest form of social activity and the most powerful kind of religious action. Through it the community participates in a mystery which confers supernatural efficacy upon its action. How this may affect social life and change the course of historical events may be seen in the rise of the Ghost Dance religion among the Indians of the Plains at the end of the nineteenth century. Here we have a well attested case of how a dance may become the medium by which the religious experience of an individual may be socialized and transmitted from one people to another with revolutionary political effects. Wovoka, an Indian of a little known and unimportant tribe in Nevada, received in a vision a dance the performance of which would bring back the spirits of their dead ancestors and the vanished herds of buffalo and the good times that were past. The dance cult spread like wildfire eastward across the mountains to the Indians of the great plains and finally stimulated the Sioux to their last desperate rising against the United States government.

The most remarkable thing about this movement was the extreme rapidity with which it communicated itself from people to people across half the continent, so that if it had not been defeated by a hopeless inequality of material power, the Ghost Dance might have changed not only the religion but also the social existence of the Indians of the Middle West in the course of a few years. Such revolutionary changes are in fact by no means rare in history. We have an example of it on the higher religious level and on a vast historical scale in the case of the rise of Islam. Here we see in full clearness and detail how a new religion may create a new culture. A single individual living in a cultural backwater originates a movement which in a comparatively short time sweeps across the world, destroying historic empires and civilizations and creating a new way of life which still moulds the thought and behaviour of millions from Senegal to Borneo. And in this case there is no common geographical environment or racial inheritance to form a basis for the spiritual community. A common faith has imposed its stamp on the most diverse human material so that the resultant product is even physically recognizable. The Arab of the desert, the West African negro, the Malay pirate, the Persian philosopher, the Turkish soldier, the Indian merchant all speak the same religious language, profess the same theological dogmas and possess the same moral values and the same social conventions. Just as Moslem architecture is different in every country but is everywhere unmistakably Moslem, so it is with this literature and speech and behaviour.

No doubt modern nationalism and secularism have altered all this, but they have done so only recently and superficially and incompletely. Islam still exists as a living culture as well as a world religion.

Thus Islam provides a classic example of how culture—the social way of life—may be transformed by a new view of life and a new religious doctrine, and how as a result social forms and institutions may be created which transcend racial and geographical limits and remain fixed for centuries. And on the other hand we have countless examples—especially among primitive peoples—of religions which are so bound up with the culture of the community that they seem to be mere psychological reflections of the way of life of a particular people in a particular environment and to possess no religious significance apart

53

from their social background. But however earthbound and socially conditioned these religions appear to be, they always look beyond society to some trans-social and superhuman reality towards which their worship is directed.

And conversely, however universal and spiritual a religion may be, it can never escape the necessity of becoming incarnated in culture and clothing itself in social institutions and traditions, if it is to exert a permanent influence on human life and behaviour.

For every historic religion from the lowest to the highest agrees on two fundamental points;—first in the belief in the existence of divine or supernatural powers whose nature is mysterious but which control the world and the life of man; and secondly in the association of these powers with particular men, or things, or places or ceremonies, which act as channels of communication or means of access between the human and the divine worlds. Thus on the lowest levels of culture we find the Shaman, the fetish, the holy place and the sacred dance, while on the higher level we have the prophet and priest, the image or sacred symbol, the temple and the sacramental liturgy. Thus every great historic culture, viewed from within through the eyes of its members, represents a theogamy, a coming together of the divine and the human within the limits of a sacred tradition.

As a rule the creative role in the formation of culture is assigned to divine or semi-divine mythical figures—culture heroes or divine ancestors—who have delivered to their descendants or followers not only the sacred myths and sacred rites of religion but the arts of life and the principles of social organization.

Sometimes these figures are themselves the creators of man, like the totemic ancestors who, as the tribes of Central Australia believe, had in the beginning journeyed through their country, performing ceremonies and leaving spirit children behind them. Sometimes they are heroic human figures which have become the centres of a cycle of myths; while the great historic cultures for the most part look back to the personality of some historical prophet or lawgiver as the source of sacred tradition or the mediator of divine revelation. And there seems to be no reason why we should exclude *a priori* the possibility of such figures arising in very primitive cultures, in the same way that Wovoka arose among the Paviotso in the nineteenth century. We must never forget that existing or recorded primitive culture is, no less than any higher civilization, the result of a long process of historical change and development, in the course of which there may have been periods of advance and regression in thought as well as in action. And though primitive culture is more communal and anonymous than the higher civilizations, it is never so communal as to exclude the creative action and influence of individual personalities. Hence the mythical figure of the first man, the culture hero, the firebearer, the teacher of the arts of life and the rites of religion is the archetype of the many forgotten or half-remembered figures which have played a decisive role in the formation or transformation of culture. In classical and oriental archaeology the progress of modern research has discovered again and again a solid bedrock of historical truth underlying the myths and legends that tradition has preserved, and in the same way behind primitive culture there is a lost world of history which is still more deeply submerged beneath the surface of consciousness.

In this twilight world history and religion are inextricably interwoven and confused, as we can see in the legends of our own past, where lost gods like Bran and Pwyll appear side by side with half-remembered historical figures like Arthur and Maxim Wledig and with the creatures of poetic legend. In

55

fact culture is like a palimpsest in which the new characters never entirely efface the old, or a patchwork in which fragments of different age and material are brought together in a single social pattern.

To the outside observer the most striking feature of primitive culture is its extreme conservatism. Society follows the same path of custom and convention with the irrational persistence of animal life.

But in reality all living culture is intensely dynamic. It is dominated by the necessity of maintaining the common life, and it is possible to ward off the forces of evil and death and gain life and good fortune and prosperity only by a continuous effort of individual and social discipline. Hence the ascetic element is prominent in primitive culture and in both primitive and advanced religions. The law of life is the law of sacrifice and discipline. If the hunter is to capture his prey, if the warrior is to overcome his enemies, if the cultivator is to receive the fruits of the earth, he must give as well as take. And he does not think of this giving in terms of manure, or drill, or athletic exercise, he views it in religious terms as sacrifice and penance and ritual acts paid to the powers above. This is the meaning of the fertility rites of the peasant culture, of the ascetic practices of the Indians of the Plains and the cult of the animal guardians among primitive hunters, all of which are keys to the understanding of their respective cultures.

So too the initiation rites, which hold so large a place in every form of culture, represent an intensive effort of social discipline directed towards the incorporation of the individual into the community under the sanction of religious powers. These are not merely ordeals of social fitness to prepare the candidate for adult life as a full member of the community, they are even more an initiation into sacred mysteries which confer new powers upon him. In some cases these initiations involve supernormal psychological experiences so that a youth's future social career may depend on the nature of his visionary experience. " Your young men shall see visions and your old men shall dream dreams." This is no more than the common experience of many an uncivilized people, and it shows how, even in lower forms of culture, religion tends to transcend the social way of life and seeks to open a path of direct access to the world above.

Thus while a culture is essentially an organized way of life, it is never conceived as a purely man-made order. The social way of life is founded on a religious law of life, and this law in turn depends on non-human powers towards which man looks with hope and fear, powers which can be known in some fashion but which remain essentially mysterious, since they are superhuman and supernatural.

Hence the relation between religion and culture is always a two-sided one. The way of life influences the approach to religion, and the religious attitude influences the way of life. Whatever is felt to be of vital importance in the life of people is brought into close relation with religion and surrounded by religious sanctions, so that every economic and social way of life has its corresponding form of religion. In so far as this is so, it is possible to construct a classification of religions based on the main sociological and economic types of culture. Thus we can distinguish the religion of the hunter, the religion of the peasant, and the religion of the warrior. Or again the religion of the tribe, the religion of the city, and the religion of the empire. These types are, of course, abstractions and cannot be applied in an exclusive or wholesale manner to the historical actuality of a particular culture. Nevertheless they are valid and useful within their proper limits and it is hardly possible to understand a particular religion without reference to them. For example the religion of the hunter is characterized by the existence of Shamans or prophets, by the dream-vision and by the cult of animal spirits, and much that appears at first sight inexplicable in the culture and religion of a people of hunters can be understood when we view it in the context of these practises and ideas. In the same way, the religion of the peasant is characterized by the worship of the Earth Mother and the cult of fertility which recur with remarkable similarities all over the world wherever the peasant culture is to be found. And since the peasant way of life underlies the higher civilizations, even when the latter are controlled by a conquering warrior people, and consciously identified with its life, we cannot understand the development of the higher religions unless we take account of the underlying stratum of peasant religion which survives as a submerged and half-forgotten element in the spiritual tradition of the culture.

All this may seem to suggest that religion is so conditioned by culture and economics that it is itself a product of culture. But however far this process of cultural conditioning goes— and it certainly may go very far—we can never exclude the alternative relation—that culture is moulded and changed by religion. It is obvious that a man's way of life is the way by which he apprehends reality—and consequently the way in which he approaches religion. Nevertheless the object of religion essentially transcends human life and the human way of life. Over against the world of human experience and social behaviour there stands the world of divine power and mystery, which is conceived by the primitive no less than by the advanced theist as essentially creative and the ultimate source of all power.

Therefore while in practice the religion of a people is limited and conditioned by its culture, in theory—and even in the theory of the primitive himself—culture is a deliberate effort to bring human life into relation with divine reality and into subordination to divine power.

58

Thus the culture process is open to change from either direction. Any material change which transforms the external conditions of life will also change the cultural way of life and thus produce a new religious attitude. And likewise any spiritual change which transforms men's views of reality will tend to change their way of life and thus produce a new form of culture.

Great cultural changes are extremely complex processes in which it is often difficult to decide the relative importance of the spiritual and material factors. But it is no more possible to deny the creative influence of new religious beliefs and doctrines, than that of new political ideas or new scientific inventions. And where the new religious influence is embodied in the personality of a great prophet or lawgiver, this creative influence of religion in cultural change is immediately evident.

No doubt great changes would have occurred in the culture of the Near East about the seventh century A.D. in any case, but that they should have taken the form they did can be explained only by the personality of Mohammed and by the doctrine he taught.

For religion, though it normally exerts a conservative influence on culture, also provides the most dynamic means of social change. Indeed one might almost go so far as to say that it is only by religion that a religious culture can be changed. The fact that a way of life has been consecrated by tradition and myth renders it singularly resistant to external change, even when the change seems obviously advantageous from a practical point of view. But if the impulse to change comes from above, from the organs of the sacred tradition itself or from some other source which claims superhuman authority, the elements in society which are most sensitive to religious impulses and most resistant to secular influences themselves become the willing agents of change.

And the creative role taken by religion in regard to culture is also to be seen in the case of those religions which at first sight seem entirely indifferent to cultural considerations. To the Western mind, for example, Buddhism has no obvious relation to culture. It appears to represent a turning of the mind away from life, in a victory of the death instinct and a denial of all the values of human culture. Nevertheless, Buddhism was emphatically a way of life, which created communities and institutions and had a more far-reaching influence on the culture of Eastern and Southern Asia than any other movement. Even to-day the Buddhist theocracy of Tibet is the most complete and imposing example of a purely religious culture existing in the modern world. And this is a remarkably interesting case, since it shows how a highly specialized way of life adapted to an exceptional environment can become fused with a very highly developed religious culture, which arose in an entirely different milieu and was imported ready-made into the utterly different social and geographical world of mediaeval Tibet. Not only was the extremely subtle and elaborate structure of Buddhist metaphysics transferred intact from Sanskrit to Tibetan, but it was later retransferred *en bloc* from Tibetan to Mongolian, so that the whole of Eastern Central Asia from the Himalayas to Lake Baikhal and Manchuria is dominated by this secondary derivative Buddhist culture which has its centre in the great monasteries of Lhasa and Tashi Llumpo and Urga. Thus by a strange irony of history the most aggressive warrior people of Asia—the Mongols—came to adopt a religion of non-aggression and universal compassion; and if, as seems probable, this event gradually led to a change in the character and habits of the people which contributed to the cessation of the age-long drive of the peoples of the steppes to East and West, it may be reckoned one of the turning points in world history.

On the other hand it is equally, or even more, clear that the native traditions of culture in Tibet and Mongolia had a powerful influence on the higher religion, so that the gods of the steppes have become members of the Buddhist pantheon and the Tibetan or Mongolian Lama is half or three-quarters a Shaman.

Here we see displayed on a colossal scale in time and space the processes of mutual interaction which are to be found everywhere at work in the relations between religion and culture. A new religion comes into contact with an old culture: it changes it and is changed by it; or a religion which has already found cultural expression in an old advanced civilization comes into contact with a primitive culture which it assimilates by communicating its own higher tradition of culture. These patterns are repeated in an endless series of variations so that they form an immense labyrinth of cultural change in which every historic culture is involved. It has been the task of the modern science of religion to unravel this tangled web and reveal the simple patterns that underly its complexities. But this rational simplification is not enough; we also need the help of a true Natural Theology to interpret the supercultural and purely religious elements that are contained in the hieroglyphs of ritual and myth. This was the older tradition of the science of religion—the tradition of the philosophers and the Fathers—and although it was discredited by the absence of a true method of historical enquiry and a lack of psychological and philological techniques, it was more true in principle than the rationalism of nineteenth century comparative religion, since it did attempt to explain religious phenomena in terms of religion—theologically, not anthropologically.

From the point of view of the theologian who studies the nature of the divine as such, there is no insuperable difficulty in the cultural differentiation of religion and the development of types of religion corresponding to the nature of the primitive cultural types. For in so far as a culture represents a natural way of life, it reflects a distinct aspect of reality and has its own particular truth and its own scale of values which provide a way of approach to transcendent truths and values, and open, as it were, a new window to heaven as well as to earth. Every way of life is therefore a potential way to God, since the life that it seeks is not confined to material satisfaction and animal activities but reaches out beyond itself towards eternal life.

The theologian teaches that every being of its nature possesses an innate tendency towards God—the natural inclination to what is absolutely universal good.

Therefore the particular goods of particular cultures are not dead ends; they are the media by which the universal good is apprehended and through which these cultures are orientated towards the good that transcends their own power and knowledge.

And thus every culture, even the most primitive, seeks, like the old Roman civic religion, to establish a *jus divinum* which will maintain the *pax deorum*, a religious order which will relate the life of the community to the transcendent powers that rule the universe. The way of life must be a way of the service of God. Otherwise it will become a way of death. This is the lesson alike of the most primitive cultures and of the highest religions, and in this agreement we find, so it seems to me, a point at which the old Natural Theology and the new scientific study of comparative religion can establish contact and find a basis of mutual understanding. Without this the study of comparative religion becomes lost in the maze of sociological relativity, and Natural Theology loses contact with religion as an historical fact.

The Sources of Religious Knowledge and the Religious Organs of Society

(I) Prophets and Divination

THE RELIGIOUS form of a culture is seen in its predominant spiritual types. For every advanced culture possesses a specialized religious class, a spiritual élite which dominates the religious tradition of society. The most primitive of these specialized types is the prophet or diviner—the man who is believed to have direct contact with the supernatural world in dreams and visions. Shamanism as the religion of the primitive hunting peoples. Social importance of visionary experience in North America. The Prophet in the higher cultures. Influence on literature. Importance of the prophetic type in times of social crisis. Islam as example of the higher type of prophetic religion. The relation between prophecy and mysticism; the two tendencies in Islam. Prophecy and charismatic leadership. The relation between Messianic prophetic movements and revolutionary social change.

The Sources of Religious Knowledge and the Religious Organs of Society

(I) PROPHETS AND DIVINATION

A FULLY developed culture involves a spiritual organization, and it is by this spiritual organization that the essential form of the culture is most clearly recognized.

For instance the three great Asiatic cultures of India, China and Islam are characterized each by its own type of spiritual élite. Thus Indian culture has been dominated by the tradition of the priestly Brahmin caste, Chinese culture by that of the Confucian scholars, and Moslem culture by the Prophets and by the Shaykhs or religious leaders who maintain the tradition of Islam.

Each of these classes is the bearer of the sacred tradition of its particular culture which is embodied in a sacred literature, a sacred philosophy and a sacred code of ritual and ceremony. Above all in each culture this class defines and canonizes the human types which are regarded as spiritual norms or ideals of moral excellence by that culture.

In all these ways, and many more, the spiritual class forms and is formed by the sacred tradition which binds the whole culture together and imprints its character upon it. This process which we see in a fully developed form in the great world cultures is to be found more or less in every society and culture.

Every social way of life in so far as it possesses a spiritual tradition and an organized social religion tends to develop this specialized religious class or order of men who are set apart and charged with the function of acting as mediators between the community and the divine world. Such classes differ, as I have said, from culture to culture, but everywhere we find the same social types recurring to such an extent that it is possible to reduce their multiplicity to a few primary archetypes.

There is first the *Priest*, who is the representative *par excellence* of the specialized religious function in society: the man who is trained and set apart to perform the rites and ceremonies—above all the sacrifices—which form the essential bond between the society and its gods, the necessary means of obtaining the divine favour.

Secondly there is the *King* or *lawgiver* who is regarded as the personal representative or embodiment of divine power. And finally there is the *Prophet* or *Seer*, the man who is the mouthpiece of the divine will, and the interpreter of dreams and oracles and the revealer of sacred mysteries.

These three types are, of course, not exclusive. The king may be a priest, or the priest may be a prophet, or the prophet may be a lawgiver. But they represent three distinct functions and thus they provide a basis for a typological classification of cultures which is of some value in the scientific study of any historical religion.

I take the prophetic type first, since it is the most important of them all from a purely religious point of view, and brings us back beneath the surface of cultural tradition and social custom to the deepest levels of religious consciousness.

Moreover the prophetic type is equally characteristic of the most primitive and the most advanced forms of religion.

Even among the lowest savages we find men who claim to have direct contact with the supernatural world in dreams and visions and are believed to make inspired utterances in a state of trance or ecstasy; while all the learning and philosophy of the higher religions are tributary and subordinated to the ultimate authority of prophetic revelation.

No doubt the Natural Theology of the eighteenth century conceived the idea of a rational religion which would dispense with the whole conception of prophetic inspiration. But this was not the traditional position of Natural Theology even in the humanist period, since the humanist exaltation or idealization of human nature found a justification in the existence of heroes and poets who transcend the limits of common experience in moments of inspiration and creative imagination. Thus the typical attitude of the religious humanist was not to reject the prophet, but rather to divinize the poet and the philosopher on the same terms.

Indeed the theory of poetic inspiration as formulated by the Platonists of the Renaissance represents a deliberate, rather sophisticated, return to the archaic conception of the poet as an inspired *vates* who spoke or rather sang under the compulsion of divine inspiration. Even the conventional invocation to the Muse and the references to poetic frenzy and the heaven-born genius which are repeated *ad nauseam* in modern European literature are the vestigial traces of a tradition far older and wider than the men of the Renaissance realized.

For as Professor and Mrs. Chadwick have shown recently with so much learning, poetry is in its origins inseparable from prophecy, and among every people we find the figure of the inspired mantic poet at the threshold of its literary tradition. "Everywhere," writes Mrs. Chadwick, "the gift of poetry is inseparable from divine inspiration. Everywhere this inspiration carries with it knowledge—whether of the past, in the form of history and genealogy; of the hidden present in the form commonly of scientific information; and of the future in the form of prophetic utterance in the narrower sense. Always this knowledge is uttered in poetry which is accompanied by music, whether of song or instrument. Music is everywhere the medium of communication with spirits. Invariably we find that the poet and seer attributes his inspiration to contact with supernatural powers, and his mood during prophetic utterance is exalted and remote from his normal existence. Generally we find that a recognized process is in vogue by which the prophetic mood can be induced at will. The lofty claims of the poet and seer are universally admitted, and he himself holds a high status wherever he is found. In addition to all this we find a common vocabulary of technical terms which go back to early times."[1]

And if this is true of primitive literature it is no less true of primitive religion. Everywhere and at all times man seeks guidance and help from the divine world, and the prophet is the natural spokesman and interpreter to men of this divine world. He is the man who dares to confront the perils of the unknown; who beholds in dreams and visions the mysteries which are veiled from common eyes, who hears the voices of spirits, and who in ecstasy and trance utters inspired oracles and warnings which guide chiefs and people in hours of decision.

There is a vast body of evidence from all ages and all cultures, from the lowest to the highest, testifying to a universal belief in prophecy. Vision and inspiration are natural to man, not in the sense that every man has them, but because every people

---

[1] N. Kershaw Chadwick. *Poetry and Prophecy* (Cassells, 1942), p. 14. So too Dr. Guillaume writes in his *Prophecy and Divination*, p. 243: " As we have seen, men have been keenly sensitive to the magic of words from the earliest times. When man first uttered rhymes and measured lines, he was thought to be imbued with magical powers. The notion that poetry is the product of inspiration was extraordinarily widespread among the peoples of antiquity. The significance of the word *carmen* among the Latins, and the belief of the Australian aborigines that their dead ancestors teach their poets their songs, are sufficient proof of the prevalence of this conception." (cf. the Arab word for poet, Shâ' ir—the knower.)

believes that there are men who have them and that such men are the chosen vehicles of the highest truth.

As a rule the higher the type of culture, the rarer and the more highly prized is this gift, so that by the time the cultural mould of a higher religion is firmly set the succession of the prophets has come to an end and the sacred canon is closed.

On the other hand, in more primitive cultures the prophetic gift is more widely diffused. Among the American Indian peoples above all, there have been tribes in which almost every normal man aspires to visionary experience and to the acquisition of supernatural powers, and as a rule it is only after prayer and fasting or other acts of mortification that he can attain his end. The religious and social implications of the ascetic experience are well shown in A. B. Skinner's account of the words in which the Iowa Shaman addresses a youth before he goes into retreat to prepare for his visionary experience. " The time has come to use the charcoal (with which the youth smears his face). Let thy tears fall on our mother, the Earth, that she may have pity on thee and help thee in thy need. Seek thy way; the Creator will help thee. He sends thee perchance a voice and prophesies to thee whether thou wilt gain renown in thy tribe or no. Perchance thou wilt dream of the thunder or of some other being above, his helper or servant. May they vouchsafe thee long life! Entreat help of the Sun. The Sun is a great power. But if there comes some power out of the water or from the earth, take it not; let it be; turn not thy attention to it. Hear nought of it; otherwise thou wilt quickly die. For so must thou hold thyself. Be cautious. There are heavenly powers and powers of evil, and these seek to deceive thee. Thou must be ready to fast, for if Wakonda helps thee, thou wilt become a great man, a protector of thy people and thou wilt obtain honour."[1]

[1] *Anthrop. Papers of the American Museum of Natural History*, XI, p. 739.

Here we see that association of social prestige and advancement with supernatural experience which is so characteristic of Shamanism in every part of the world, and most of all in America. But there is also a strong emphasis on spiritual values which are not of social origin, a consciousness of the supernatural dangers that beset the spiritual journey and of the need for the discernment of spirits. And when we come to the greater figures which this culture has produced—to the prophet of the Delawares who inspired Pontiac, to the brother of Tecumseh, the Shawnee prophet, who took for himself the name Tenkswatawa, " The Open Door ", to Kanakuk, the Kickapoo prophet of the early seventeenth century, or to Wovoka, the Paviotso prophet, we see how under the stress of national disaster this barbaric type of prophetic religion was capable of producing a series of Messianic leaders who attempted to save their people by moral and religious reformation of their culture.

This kind of development is not confined to North America, it is in fact the normal reaction of the prophetic type of religion whenever the culture is threatened by alien influences; as we see in South Africa, in the Sudan and in New Zealand, during the nineteenth century. Under more favourable conditions, however, the prophetic development may take a non-political direction so that the prophet becomes concerned with religious teaching rather than with social action. More often, however, it is the lower and more utilitarian functions of divination and the interpretation of omens that suppress the higher aspects of the prophet's activity, so that he becomes a " medicine man " or " witch doctor " or magician.

But even so there is the possibility of a higher power intruding on the socialized and semi-secularized technique of the diviner, as we see in the great story of Balaam, where the professional diviner, hired by the king to lay a curse on the enemies of his tribe, is transformed against his will into the inspired prophet who reveals the divine oracles

> *—The Man whose eye was closed saith*
> *He saith, who heareth the words of God*
> *Who seeth the vision of the Almighty*
> *Falling down and having his eyes open—*

For the primitive prophet or seer stands midway between the mystic and the medium. On the one hand, any kind of ecstasy or trance or state of dissociation is regarded as supernatural, and the ravings of a psychotic are treated with religious reverence. But on the other hand, since primitive culture recognizes vision and inspiration as the highest kind of knowledge and accords such high honour to the man who possesses these gifts, the prophetic class will be a true spiritual élite which will include the best and the most religious elements in the society, as well as the more extraordinary or abnormal types.

And this combination of elements which seem to us anomalous or contradictory is to be found on a far higher level of culture in the religious orders or confraternities of Islam whose leaders have included the greatest mystics, like Jalaluddin Rumi[1] or Abd al Qadir al Jilani,[2] while descending at the other end of the scale to the crudest practices of autohypnosis and orgiastic excitement.

In fact the prophetic type covers the whole range of religious experience and spiritual achievement from the saint and the mystic through the visionary and the dreamer down to the medium and the diviner—from those great souls whom

---

[1] Maulana Jalaluddin Rumi, the great Persian poet and Moslem saint, was born at Balkh in 1207 and died in 1273 at Konich in Asia Minor where he founded the famous order of the Mevlevi dervishes of which his descendants have been the heads ever since.

[2] Abd al Qadir al Jilani (d. 1166), the founder of the Qadirite order and one of the greatest and most popular of Moslem saints. His tomb at Bagdad is still a great place of pilgrimage.

humanity has worshipped as mirrors of the divine perfection down to Mr. Sludge the medium and the savage witch doctor.

We see this confusion of higher and lower elements clearly enough in the history of Greek religion where the prophetic element was always strong and showed itself in the highly institutionalized system of the Delphic oracle as well as in the orgiastic Dionysian religion and the mystical Orphic cult. But above all it finds its highest expression in Greek philosophy itself, which in its origins was a kind of prophecy and followed the traditional patterns of mantic poetry and revelation.

The most striking representative of this prophetic philosophy is Heracleitus who not only deliberately chose an oracular form of utterance but was filled with a profound sense of prophetic mission and prophetic inspiration.[1]

I will say no more of this aspect of the Greek religious tradition at the moment, since in spite of its importance for the history of thought, it cannot be regarded as typical of prophetic religion. It is in the Semitic world rather than in the West that the classical type of prophetic religion is to be found, and it is there that the relation between the religious institution of prophecy and the social order of culture is most fully exemplified.

This Semitic prophetism has been to a certain extent incorporated into our own religious tradition through the Old

[1] In her recent *Companion to the Pre-Socratic Philosophers*, Miss K. Freeman writes as follows (p. 121):

" There was, however, one kind of supernatural manifestation of which Heracleitus approved: oracular responses. He speaks in the highest terms both of the Delphic Oracle and of the Sibyl. He believed, therefore, in prophecy, and that suitable instruments could be used by divine powers to make known the future. It seems likely that he regarded himself as a teacher of this kind, and found the oracular utterance best suited for what he wished to express. Respect for the Delphic Oracle became a tradition in philosophic thought; and it persisted at a time when belief in Delphi was waning, and attacks on it were becoming fierce. Socrates professed implicit trust in the gods, though Euripides' *Ion* shows how far scepticism had gone by the end of the fifth century; and Plato still gives Delphi a place of honour in his Republic."

Testament and the bond between the religion of Israel and Christianity. But the continuity of prophetic religion is also preserved in its original Semitic environment in the tradition of Islam which is the religion of the Prophet *par excellence*.

Hence this field of religious phenomena can be studied as a whole in the history of Islam even better than in primitive culture or than in our own, for Islamic culture has always been more concerned than that of the West with the specific nature of the prophetic gift, and at the same time it has been more at home in that primitive underworld of magic and divination, the existence of which has been almost forgotten by the philosophers and theologians of the West.

In contrast to the Greeks and to the peoples who created the archaic culture, the Semitic peoples in historic times were not deeply concerned with the problem of the order of nature. They saw the world in a more primitive fashion as a battlefield of contending forces—of superhuman powers which had to be placated and obeyed rather than controlled and understood. The Semitic background was not the world of the Mediterranean where the gods are the friends of man and crown his labour with the vine and the olive, but the world of the desert in which man exists only on sufferance and is always at the mercy of alien powers. In such a world there is little room for rational calculation, and life is ruled by fate and chance and personal luck and prowess. And the wise man does not trust too much to his own prowess but looks for help to supernatural guidance and warnings, to divination and to an implicit obedience to an incomprehensible divine will. No doubt the Semites have occupied the old centres of the archaic culture; they have built cities and founded kingdoms and empires. But it is not here that the dynamic force of their culture is to be found: the roots of their spiritual life are elsewhere. Again and again the wind blows from the desert and a new movement

73

of prophetic inspiration comes to overturn kingdoms and bring new life into the settled cultures.

This historic role of prophecy and prophetic movements as a recurrent factor in Semitic culture has been explicitly recognized by Islamic thought. In particular, Ibn Khaldun the famous Arabic historian who wrote in North Africa in the later fourteenth century (1332-1406) bases his whole theory of history on the dynamic influence of successive prophetic movements so that his theory of prophecy is closely bound up with his theory of sociological and cosmic change.[1]

The world, he says, is an endless process of change in which the successive levels of existence are joined to one another and change into those which are beyond them upwards and downwards so that the last degree of each region of existence is fitted to become the beginning of the region that comes after it.

In this hierarchy of existence man represents the last degree of the region of animal existence and the beginning of a higher world of spiritual existence. " This is the beginning of a region which extends from man onwards and here ends that which we can directly observe."

The human soul therefore has contact with the regions beyond it like the other ordered existences. And these contacts are in two directions—downwards through the body into the world of sense, and upwards through the mind into the world of spirits. There are souls which through their weakness are confined to the knowledge of the sensible world and to those fields of knowledge which are accessible to the imagination and the discursive reason. And there are souls which are capable of a purely spiritual apprehension and of transcending the sensible and imaginative knowledge of particular things. And finally there are the souls which possess the power of

[1] Ibn Khaldun's philosophy of history is contained in his *Muqaddama*, composed in 1377, translated by W. McGuckin de Slane under the title *Prolegomènes*, 3 vols., 1863-8, cf. especially vol. I, pp. 184-220.

passing from the human to the spiritual world, so that they become temporarily pure spirits and hear spiritual speech and receive divine inspiration. These are the Prophets whom God has created to be a means of access between Him and His creatures to instruct men and guide them in the way of salvation.

And these consequently are the ultimate sources of creative change in history and in the world of man, just as the soul moves the body, and the spiritual world changes the world of inanimate matter. Such prophets are rare, and it is only painfully and with difficulty that they attain the moment of vision and the flash of inspiration.

Nevertheless the capacity of vision, the power of passing over from the material to the spiritual world exists potentially in human nature as a whole.

Therefore we may expect to find a series of intermediate degrees between the prophet, the purely spiritual man, and the lowest type which is completely immersed in the world of sense. In this intermediate region Ibn Khaldun places all those phenomena of divination and clairvoyance and autohypnosis which are so characteristic of the primitive Shaman and which retained much of their importance and prestige in mediaeval Islamic society. These, he argues, are also signs of man's spiritual nature, imperfect forms of inspiration which are not extricated, as in the case of the prophet, from the power of the senses and the imagination.

The highest of these forms of inspiration of which this class of men is capable is attained by the aid of rhymed or rhythmic speech by which the diviner may be diverted from the senses and strengthened in some degree for his limited attainment of the spiritual. And still lower than these are the common sort of diviners or mediums who require some sensible object or image to stimulate their inspiration or intuitive faculty.

Finally the simplest and most rudimentary expression of the faculty of vision and one that is common to all men is that which occurs in dreams, when the activity of the senses is temporarily suspended by sleep, without any deliberate intention or control on the part of the dreamer.

In this state, says Ibn Khaldun, the spirit withdraws from the external senses and returns to its internal powers and to the forms that are stored in the memory, and thence it derives by combination and selection these imaginary forms that the dreamer apprehends. Sometimes however the soul may turn aside for a moment to its spiritual essence in spite of the resistance of its internal powers and perceive forms by spiritual intuition, because it is so created—then the imagination takes these forms and presents them as they essentially are, or clothes them in imaginary forms of a symbolic character. And thus there are three types of dream, which correspond to the three types of spiritual nature.

There is the confused and meaningless dream which is due to the uncontrolled activity of the mind working on the forms that are stored in its memory without any deeper background of spiritual apprehension; secondly there is the symbolic dream, in which the sensible image has a symbolic or analogous relation to some higher spiritual idea which can be discovered by analysis and interpretation; and finally there is the true dream which carries immediate conviction in a flash of spiritual knowledge and which therefore is more akin in its nature to genuine prophetic inspiration than anything else in man's normal experience.

This is a very brief and inadequate summary of Ibn Khaldun's position, but it suffices to show the remarkable way in which he integrates all the diverse phenomena of prophecy, inspiration and divination with his system of thought which is essentially that of a Natural Theologian. For Ibn Khaldun

76

occupies an almost unique central position not only midway between East and West, but also between the modern scientific approach and the naïve and receptive attitude of primitive culture. From the purely religious point of view, however, he is surpassed by another great Moslem philosopher, Al Ghazali (1058–1111), a thinker who studied the same problems with no less subtlety and with even greater profundity and intuition. For Al Ghazali was himself a religious genius of the first order, like St. Augustine, who did not study religious phenomena from without but wrote of the things that he had known, under the influence of a life-changing experience.[1]

No philosopher has, in fact, had a clearer realization of the limits of reason and of the impossibility of communicating by logical argument the essential nature of the spiritual realities with which religion is necessarily and directly concerned. Yet, at the same time, nothing could be more decisive than his rejection of the purely traditionalist attitude that has been so common in Islam. " There is no hope," he writes, " in returning to a traditional faith after it has once been abandoned, since the essential condition in the holder of a traditional faith is that he should not know he is a traditionalist. Whenever he knows that the glass of his traditional faith is broken; that is a breaking that cannot be mended, and a separating that cannot be united by any sewing or putting together, except it be melted in the fire and given another new form."[2]

Religious truth, therefore, cannot be discovered by philosophy or taught by tradition. It can be found only by that direct

[1] There is a good sketch of Al Ghazali's life and personality in *Al Ghazali the Mystic* by Margaret Smith (London, 1944). Most of my quotations are from his history of his spiritual and intellectual development—*Al Mungidh min al Dalal*—a book, writes D. B. Macdonald, " which is unique in Arabic for the keenness and fullness of its self-revelation." Where possible, I have quoted Dr. Macdonald's translation.

[2] Tr. D. B. Macdonald, *The Religious Life and Attitude in Islam*, p. 180 (Chicago, 1909).

vision of spiritual reality which is the prophetic experience. " A man who has not this experience cannot know what it is like and can hardly conceive of its possibility, just as a man who has been born blind cannot understand what is meant by colour.

" It is impossible to believe in prophecy without admitting the existence of this spiritual intuition. For to believe in the prophet is to admit that there is above reason a sphere in which there are revealed to the inner vision truths beyond the grasp of reason, just as things seen are not apprehended by the sense of hearing nor things understood by that of touch." Any other view reduces the prophet to the level of a wise man who is the instructor of men and thus turns religion into philosophy.

Thus the true spiritual knowledge which is the science of the saints is derived from the light of the lamp of prophecy. " And other than the light of prophecy there is none on the face of the earth from which illumination may be sought."[1] At every period and under every dispensation such illuminated men have existed. " God does not deprive this world of them, for they are its sustainers and they draw down to it the blessings of heaven, according to the tradition; ' it is by them that you obtain rain, it is by them that you receive your subsistence.' "

Whatever of spiritual truth is to be found in human philosophy and in human religions is derived from this source, alloyed and corrupted by the vain tradition and reasonings of men. But the man who leaves human reasoning and follows the way of the saints by cleansing the mind from all that is not God and advancing in prayer and spiritual perfection comes at last to that supreme intuition of divine reality which cannot be defined in logical terms or described in words, but of which we can only say with the poet

[1] *op cit.*, p. 186.

" And there happened what happened of that which I mention not;
So think of a good thing and ask not concerning the Good."

" He who has not been granted actual experience of anything
of this can know of the essence of prophecy only the name.
For the wonders of the saints are in reality the beginnings of
prophets."[1]

Hence " the prophets are the physicians of the diseases of the
soul and the only use and authority for reason is that it should
teach us this and should bear witness to the truth of prophecy
and to its own inability to attain to what the eye of prophecy
can reach. And that it should take us by our hand and commit
us to prophecy as the blind are committed to their guides
and the sick to their physicians. This is the work and bound
of reason and beyond this it cannot go except to make known
what the physician has taught it."[2]

In this way Al Ghazali bases his apologetic on the fact of
prophecy and the non-rational character of religious experience
as directly and drastically as any philosopher of religion has
ever done.

At first sight, therefore, his position seems diametrically
opposed to all that we understand by natural theology—not
only to the theological rationalism of his great adversary
Averroes but also to the Natural Theology of St. Thomas whom
Don Miguel Asín Palacios regards as his disciple.[3]

Nevertheless since Al Ghazali practically identifies prophecy
with mystical intuition and regards the latter as an innate
faculty of the human soul, he ultimately arrives at a natural
theology of a very mystical kind.

[1] *op. cit.*, p. 187.
[2] Tr. *op. cit.*, p. 192.
[3] cf. M. Asin Palacios *El Averroismo teológico de S. Tomás de Aquino*
1904.

Nor is his theory at bottom any more irrational than that of the physical scientist. No less than the scientist he appeals to experience and experimental proofs. In fact Al Ghazali himself draws attention to the similarity of the two cases, and points out that both astronomy and medicine depend not on abstract reasoning but on the observation of facts and states which may lie quite beyond the range of our ordinary experience, as for example in the case of astronomical phenomena which occur only at very rare intervals.

In the same way the fact that prophecy and inspiration and the higher forms of spiritual intuition are rare phenomena outside our common experience does not mean that they are incredible or unreal. The highest knowledge may be the rarest knowledge and yet at the same time the supreme standard of reality and truth. And what then is the value of a religious theory which rules out the witness of the saints, or a metaphysical system which shuts its eyes to the sources of spiritual truth? Is it not as fundamentally irrational as a physical science which refuses to study the facts of nature and contents itself with text books, abstract argument and logical definitions?

I have discussed the views of Al Ghazali at some length not only because he is a classical exponent of the prophetic type of religion who has exercised an enormous influence on the religious development of one of the great world cultures, but also because he possessed a highly cultivated and critical intelligence and was fully conscious of the implications of his religious theory and the objections to which it was exposed.

" For," says he, " a thirst to comprehend the true essences of things was from my earliest days my characteristic idiosyncrasy, a natural gift of God and a disposition that he had implanted in my nature, by no choice or devising of my own; until there was loosed from me the bond of conformity and my inherited beliefs were broken down when I was yet but little more than a lad."

Yet for all his scepticism and intellectual curiosity, Al Ghazali gave a much larger place to the facts of religious experience and prophetic inspiration than did the orthodox traditionalists and scholastics, who represent the other and older trend in Islamic thought. For he regarded the prophetic experience not as a remote and isolated fact, but as the most outstanding example of the direct spiritual vision which is common to the mystics and the saints and is accessible to every man called to the way of perfection and the contemplative life.

Nevertheless in spite of the sharp opposition of these two tendencies—represented on the one hand by the mysticism of the Dervish confraternities and on the other by the traditionalism of the puritan sects—they are both at one in this acceptance of the prophetic experience as the basic and essential religious fact.

Nor is this peculiar to Islam. For almost all the controversies that have raged between theologians on the argument from religious experience are ultimately reducible to the difference between the traditionalists who appeal to the unique authority of a particular prophetic inspiration and the mystics who claim a direct approach to spiritual vision by the way of asceticism and the contemplative life. It is only a non-religious philosophy which denies *in toto* the validity of religious experience.

And in so far as religious experience is essential to religion, the prophetic type, either in the wider or more restricted sense, is the universal, necessary and fundamental organ of religion. In every religion the religious aim of a culture is determined by the mission and the inspiration of its prophets and by the vision and spiritual experience of its mystics. Where these vital organs fail, religion becomes secularized and is absorbed in the cultural tradition to a point at which it becomes identified with it, until it finally becomes nothing more than a form of social activity, perhaps even a servant or accomplice of the powers of this world.

No doubt this degradation of religion may occur within the prophetic organ itself, as in the case of the false prophets, against whom Jeremiah wrote: " A wonderful and horrible thing has come to pass in the land; the prophets prophesy falsely and the priests bear rule by their means; and my people love to have it so: and what will ye do in the end thereof? "

The characteristic danger of prophecy as a socio-religious institution is not, however, the tendency to excessive social conformity, but an excess of individualism, and its liability to become the channel for all sorts of disruptive, revolutionary and anti-social forces.

We see this often enough in the history of Islam from the time of al-Muqanna, the veiled prophet of Khurasan, and Babak the Khurammite in the eighth and ninth centuries down to the Sudanese Mahdi in the later nineteenth century. And elsewhere throughout history it is possible to trace a continuous relation between revolutionary and prophetic movements. There are the Taborites in Bohemia, the Anabaptists at Munster in 1534, the Fifth Monarchy Men in seventeenth-century England and countless more forgotten leaders of lost causes who have claimed a divine commission to avenge social injustice and establish the millennial kingdom of Christ and His saints. Nor is this prophetic element entirely absent from the modern revolutionary movement, in spite of its profoundly secular character. Rousseau himself is a remarkable example of the secularized prophetic type, and the leaders of the French Revolution, above all Robespierre and St. Just, were the Khalifas of this humanitarian Mahdi.

Even in the nineteenth century, although Lamennais and Victor Hugo and many lesser men were prophets manqués, who failed to arouse any real religious enthusiasm, the movement of social revolution as a whole undoubtedly owed much of its power to non-political and non-economic forces which had their origin on the deeper levels of consciousness. And thus we have seen the strange paradox of the Marxian movement which has so many of the characteristics of a new prophetic religion in spite of its materialist ideology and its secularist ethics.

This disassociation of the Messianic or charismatic principle in revolutionary movements from its religious background is not peculiar to Marxism. We have seen the same thing happening in the case of German National Socialism, where the principle of charismatic leadership was deliberately used in order to mobilize the unconscious forces that lie dormant in civilized man and transform them into instruments of power. There is in truth nothing new in the attempt to exploit religious passions for the sake of power, and if orthodox historians are to be believed, the *du'at* of the Ismailians and the Assassins[1] in the Middle Ages were as unscrupulous and ruthless in their revolutionary propaganda as the agents of any modern totalitarian party. What is new is the discovery that this exploitation of the subterranean forces of the collective unconscious is still as possible in a rationalized, scientific, secular culture as it was in a religious society. When the prophets are silent and society no longer possesses any channel of communication with the divine world, the way to the lower depths is still open and man's frustrated spiritual powers will find their outlet in the unlimited will to power and destruction.

In the past man has been very conscious of this danger and

---

[1] The Ismailian branch of the Shiites set up the Opposition Khalifate of the Fatimids in North Africa and Egypt and carried on an immense underground movement against orthodox Islam throughout the East from the ninth to the thirteenth century. This movement gave birth to the " New Propaganda " of terrorism organised by Hasan-i-Sabbah and the order or party of the Assassins which had its centre at Alamut in Persia and Banias in Syria, from the end of the eleventh century to 1256 when Alamut was destroyed by the Mongols.

he has attempted to protect himself by fortifying the original deposit of prophetic revelation with all the authority of social tradition and institutional forms. Thus Islam, the typical prophetic religion, is also a classical example of traditionalism, so that any saying of the Prophet and the companions of the Prophet, every action, custom and decision, has been recorded and commented and built into the vast fabric of orthodox theology and canon law. Here the revolutionary force of the prophetic movement has acted as a stabilizing influence on the later development of Islam, as the molten lava that flows from the volcano becomes harder and more durable than any common rock.

As a rule, however, the prophet does not stand alone as the sole spiritual organ of a developed culture. His office is counterbalanced by that of the priesthood which normally acts as the authoritative, regulating principle in religion and the institutional bond between religion and culture. Islam is almost unique in its subordination of priesthood to prophecy and even here the Ulema—the class of theologians and canon lawyers—hold a very important place in Moslem culture.

In the other world religions, and still more in the polytheistic religions of the archaic cultures, such as those of Mesopotamia, Asia Minor, and Central America—the priesthood has become the primary religious organ of society and has absorbed or subordinated the prophetic office. Where this tendency reaches its extreme development, however, as in the religion of ancient Rome, the priesthood loses its religious vitality and becomes a purely social institution—a sort of honorary ornamental magistracy. When this point is reached, the living spiritual elements in society turn away from the official religion either to a negative form of prophecy which denies religion like that of Lucretius, or to some new source of revelation which springs up like a fountain in the desert.

The Sources of Religious Knowledge and the Religious Organs of Society

(II) Priesthood and Sacrifice

PRIESTHOOD as the typical cultural organ of religion. Its importance as a culture-building institution. The priesthood as the first professional learned class. Its close connection with the rise of the archaic culture in Mesopotamia and elsewhere. The temple as the focus of civic life. The priest as ritual specialist and master of the sacrifice. Primitive conceptions of the social and cosmic functions of sacrifice. Classical development of these conceptions in Indian religion. Transition from ritual technology to religious metaphysics. The Vedanta as the fulfilment and transcending of the ritual order. Buddhism as a reaction against the doctrine of the sacrifice and the domination of the priesthood. Yet the Buddhist monastic order is the heir of the Brahmin tradition. The world-denying tendencies of Buddhism do not prevent its having an influence on culture, and Buddhist monasticism is itself a great cultural institution. Tendency of Buddhism to revert to the older traditions. General intellectual tendencies of the institution of priesthood. Relations between clergy and intelligentsia in Western culture.

The Sources of Religious Knowledge and the Religious Organs of Society

(II) PRIESTHOOD AND SACRIFICE

I

OF ALL the, social organs of religion the priesthood is that which has the most direct and enduring influence on culture. For priesthood represents religion embodied in a stable institution which forms an integral part of the structure of society and assumes a corporate responsibility for the religious life of the community.

Hence the immense importance of the priesthood as a culture-building institution; for in ancient times it was the only institution which was culturally self-conscious and possessed the power to control the whole social way of life and guide it towards an ultimate spiritual aim.

For the priest is not only the religious leader of the community. He is also the guardian of its sacred traditions and the master of a sacred technique.

From the beginning, the relations between the community and the divine powers were regarded as a matter which demanded expert knowledge and technical training. Side by side with the inspired utterances of the prophet, there were the sacred formulas and rites which were the province of the priest. Such formulas and rites are to be found in the most primitive forms of culture known to us, and, with the development of civilization, they grew in number and complexity, until they eventually formed the subject matter of an immense systematized body of knowledge which was the sole preoccupation of a learned and powerful class.

The existence of a class of this kind is closely bound up with the origins of civilization, for the earliest known forms of higher culture in Mesopotamia and Egypt already possessed powerful and highly organized priesthoods. Nor is this exceptional, for the same development is to be found in every centre of archaic culture in both the Old and the New Worlds from Egypt to Yucatan; while the secondary and possibly derivative cultures of a less highly developed type—as in Polynesia, West Africa, New Mexico and Florida—show a parallel development on a lower plane.

Viewed as a whole, this sacerdotal type of culture must be regarded as the central tradition of world civilization on which all existing forms of higher culture depend or from which they derive. The earliest centres of this culture in the Near East—in Mesopotamia and Syria, in Egypt and in Crete—were in contact with one another from prehistoric times; and already in the third millennium B.C. the whole of this area was becoming a civilized *orbis terrarum* in which the different centres of civilization were in relation with one another and influenced and stimulated each other's development both materially and intellectually. Some contact and a very considerable parallelism of development existed between this focus of civilization and the contemporary centre of archaic culture in the Indus valley, the existence of which has only recently been discovered.

And though the development of the archaic civilization in North China seems to be much more recent, there is reason to believe that it is related to the same movement of culture and owed much (though we do not know how much) to the slow penetration of influences from the West. On the other hand

88

there is no satisfactory evidence that the cultures of the New World had any contact with or dependence upon those of the Old. Nevertheless the Maya culture in Central America is a typical example of the sacerdotal culture, and shows a remarkable resemblance in several respects to those of the Old World, so that it would seem as though this sacerdotal phase was not merely characteristic of a particular historical development but was an indispensable condition for the appearance of a higher culture in any part of the world and in any age.

Thus the essential feature of this archaic civilization is the existence of a learned priesthood whose predominance gave the whole culture a markedly theocratic character. In most cases the society found its centre in a sacred city and a city temple, the god of which was the ruler and owner of the land. The service of the gods provided the ritual setting and pattern by which the life of the community was ordered.

In Mesopotamia such temple cities were already in existence in the fourth millennium B.C., and the earliest tablets discovered at Urukh beneath the great temple of the Mother Goddess prove that even at this period the temple had become at once a centre of economic organization and a centre of learning. The rise of these wealthy and learned temple corporations which possessed archives and schools and all the apparatus of scholarship was of decisive importance for the history of culture, since it opened the way to the systematic accumulation of knowledge and the cultivation of science and literature.

But it was of no less importance for religion, since the rise of the priesthood created a principle of social organization within the religious sphere and tended to substitute an ordered system of hierarchical relations for the individual and incalculable activities of the prophet, the Shaman and the magician. The more this principle of organization is developed, the closer

89

become the relations between ritual law and mythology and doctrine, until they are finally integrated in a more or less coherent system.

This integration involves a still higher degree of intellectual training and specialization, so that the great temple cities, like Heliopolis and Memphis in Egypt or Ur, Lagash and Nippur in Mesopotamia became centres of learning, in which mathematical and astronomical science, as well as theology and ritual, were cultivated systematically.

II

Nevertheless the primary function of the priest is not to teach. It is to offer sacrifice. The sacrifice is the vital bond of communion between the people and its gods; and the priest is the master of the sacrifice.

No doubt in its origins sacrifice may seem one of the simplest and most spontaneous of all religious acts, so much so indeed that it has often been taken in the past as a criterion of natural religion. Thus St. Augustine asserts on the one hand the universality of sacrifice—" there is no people without sacrifice "—and on the other the essential relation of sacrifice to the idea of God—" No man offers sacrifice to any being whom he does not hold to be divine."

But with the development of priesthood as an organized social institution, the simple act of sacrifice becomes transformed into a solemn and mysterious rite which gathers round it a whole complex of practices and ideas, often of a very abstruse character, until finally a theory of sacrifice is developed which becomes as important as, or more important than, theology itself, the theory of the nature of the gods.

At the same time the sacrifice may become a centre round which mythological concepts are crystallized and organized.

The first of St. Augustine's propositions is still practically undisputed by students of religion, but the second is more controversial, since the evidence of primitive culture suggests that there is a relation between sacrifice and the magical ceremonies connected with the increase of the food supply which are not necessarily addressed to a divine being. The best known example of this is the *intichiuma* ceremonies of the Central Australian tribes which are concerned with the multiplication of the totemic animals or plants, and similar though less highly developed rites connected with the food supply are to be found amongst many other peoples at many different levels of culture, as for example in the hunting magic of the American Indians and the fertilization rites of peasant peoples. In all such cases the offering and the ceremony are means by which man participates in the mysterious process of nature, and evokes and stimulates its creative forces.

Whenever there is a developed conception of the nature of the divine powers, the offering is conceived as a sacrifice to the gods, but where this is not the case, the rite is still performed as a sacred mystery through which man enters into communion with the unknown and impersonal sources of life.

The institution of priesthood has therefore a twofold origin. On the one hand, the priest is the servant of the god, the minister of the temple and the diviner who ascertains the divine will and decree. On the other hand, he is the master of the sacrifice without whose power and knowledge the sacred rites cannot be performed. He is the bridge builder and the guardian of the threshold between the world of men and the world of the gods. It is in his power to open and close the channels by which divine blessings are conferred on the community so that he himself comes to share in some measure in the power and prestige of the gods.

III

The most remarkable example of this specialized development of sacrificial and ritual technique is to be found in the religious culture of India which possesses a unique and unbroken tradition, reaching back to prehistoric times. Already thousands of years ago this sacerdotal tradition had been codified in an elaborate system which even in its earliest recorded form possesses an aura of immemorial antiquity. And it is of outstanding importance not only on account of its antiquity, and the wealth of documentation that we possess, but still more on account of the intensity and persistence with which this particular line of development was pursued. Nowhere is the conception of the priest as master of the sacrifice worked out with such elaboration of detail and with such ingenuity of speculative theory. Poetry and mythology, ritual and magic, education and law, philosophy and mysticism, are all interwoven in an elaborate pattern which centres in the sacrifice and is controlled and ordered by the priesthood. From the primitive conception of the magical potency of the sacred formula there develops the speculative theory of the creative power of the divine word—the Brahman; until finally we reach the conscious philosophical identification of the enlightened mind, with the Atman—the self—with Brahman, the ultimate basis of all things and the sole transcendent supersubstantial Reality.

Now the whole of this development from beginning to end is dominated by the theory of the sacrifice. It is the sacrifice that makes the sun rise and controls the course of the seasons. It is by the sacrifice that the gods live, and it is for the sacrifice that men exist, and through the sacrifice that they acquire wealth and success in life and power and knowledge, that reach beyond life and beyond the gods, until they penetrate to the innermost mystery of being.

But this development cannot be interpreted as a straight-forward progress from magic to religion or from mythology to mysticism. On the contrary, the religious element is more pronounced in the religious poetry of the Rig Veda[1] than in the ritual technology of the Brahmanas. Yet the magnificent religious poetry of the hymns of the Rig Veda is subsidiary to the technique of the sacrifice, and the fantastic magical speculation of the Brahmanas is inextricably bound up with the sublime metaphysical intuition of the Upanishads.

This theological development of the theory of the sacrifice is intimately related to the sociological development of the institution of priesthood, which in India as nowhere else was able to concentrate the whole intellectual and social energy of the community on the intensive cultivation and study of its specialized functions. It is indeed a most remarkable example of what may happen when a spiritual élite is allowed to develop freely as in a vacuum without social criticism or control.

And it is the more remarkable, since the Indian priestly class was not based, as in Mesopotamia and Egypt, on the corporate organization of a temple priesthood. For the Brahmin was essentially a household priest and it was as the domestic chaplain (purohita) of a chief or king that he acquired social prestige and wealth. Consequently the Vedic sacrifice was not an official civic act like the temple sacrifices of the archaic city state. It had a more individualistic character, since it was always directed to the interests of some particular

[1] The Rig Veda, the earliest religious literature of India, is the great collection of hymns, forming part of the sacrificial liturgy. The Brahmanas are prose treatises on ritual as taught in the great Vedic schools, and the Upanishads consist of mystical or philosophic discussions, originally appended to the Brahmanas and dealing with their esoteric significance. In addition to the Rig Veda, there were also the Sama Veda, containing the verses chanted at the soma sacrifice, the Yajur Veda which contains the sacrificial formulae, and the Atharva Veda, a later collection of incantations and spells which is less liturgical and more popular in character than the three older Vedas.

person at whose expense the ceremony was performed. The essential social relation was not that of the temple and the state as in the Near East, but that of the Brahmin and his patron. Indeed the attitude of the poet-priests of the Rig Veda is not unlike that of Pindar towards the wealthy and well born gentlemen who financed his victory odes.

At first sight this seems an unpromising starting point for the quest of the absolute eternal reality, and there is an enormous gulf between the extroverted polytheism of the Rig Veda with its naïve wholehearted desire for wealth, long life and victory, and the *via negativa* expounded by the great sages and ascetics of the Upanishads. Nevertheless we can trace every step of the transformation in Vedic literature and it is by the dialectic of the sacrifice that it was achieved.

Already in the earliest period, we find the divine elements of the sacrifice, Agni and Soma, the Sacred Fire and the Sacred Libation, being worshipped on an equality with the great native gods of the Vedic pantheon. Agni is fire—he is the household fire, the friend and protector of the family—he is the sacrificial fire, the father of sacrifice, the lord of prayer, the giver of all good gifts, the father of immortality—he is the cosmic fire who is born in heaven, on earth, and in the waters, the begetter of the two worlds, who has filled heaven and earth and the great sun. But Agni is also the Priest, the Purohita of the Gods, the Hotri of the Two Worlds who nourishes and sustains the gods and heaven and earth by the ceaseless cycle of sacrifice. Hence he is the priesthood itself—the Brahman—and the human priest is his human embodiment and co-efficient, as we see in the sacrificial formula " Thou, O Agni, art kindled by Agni, priest as thou art, by a priest, friend by friend."[1]

Thus we find side by side in the Vedas, the practical utili-

[1] Satapatha Brahmana XII, iv. 3. 5. (Sacred Books of the East XLIV, p. 189.)

tarianism of the " *do ut des* " theory of sacrifice expressed in its crudest form—" Here is butter, give me cows "; and on the other hand, a growing sense of the cosmic significance of sacrifice as an act of mystical communion by which the priest participates in the mystery of creation. By degrees a vast system of dramatic symbolism grew up round the sacrifice which reached its culmination in the symbolism of the great Fire Altar, the construction of which is described in such minute detail in Books VI to X of the Satapatha Brahmana—perhaps the most elaborate ceremony recorded in any religious document.

Here the altar represents at once the structure of the universe, the corpus of the Vedas and the body of the divine creator and victim; and when the ceremony has been completed and the sacrifice offered, the priest restores the unity of creation and brings back life to the dismembered body of the Lord of Creatures.

IV

The development of this elaborate system of ritual symbolism inevitably tended to displace the centre of religious gravity from the anthropomorphic figures of the gods to the sacred mystery of the sacrifice as an impersonal cosmic divine act, so that eventually the power of sacrifice took the place of the object of sacrifice as the ultimate divine reality. In this sense Brahman signifies the mystical or magic power which is immanent in both the priest and the sacrifice and finds its most direct expression in the sacred formula and the inspired word of the Vedas. And as the attention of the priesthood became concentrated on this central mystery, they became increasingly aware of the importance of mind and thought in the *opus divinum*. As the chief priest, who is named Brahman *par excellence*, sits apart in silence and recollection overseeing the work of the other priests and directing the work in spirit and knowledge, so in the cosmic process it is Brahman, the All-knowing and the All-pervading, from whose brooding contemplation arise the world of the gods and the world of creatures, and in whom is Eternal Being, Eternal Knowledge and Eternal Bliss.

With the coming of this knowledge, the ritual science of the priesthood gave birth to a true natural theology, for the first time in world history. But the development did not stop at this point. For almost simultaneously the teachers of Brahman attained the intuition of the identity of the Brahman, which is the soul of the universe, with the Self of the thinker. This is the fundamental doctrine of the Upanishads " Whoever knows this—*Aham Brahma asmi*—I am Brahma—becomes the All. Even the Gods are not able to prevent him from becoming it. For he becomes their Self."[1]

This was a revolutionary event in the history of Indian religion, for at one stroke it rendered superfluous the immense structure of ritual science and ceremonial observance which had accumulated round the sacrifice and which was beginning to be felt as a burden too heavy to be borne.

" Such indeed," says the Satapatha Brahmana, " are the wilds and ravines of sacrifice and they take hundreds upon hundreds of days' journeyings; and if any venture into them without knowledge, then hunger or thirst, evil doers and fiends harass them, even as fiends would harass foolish men wandering in a wild jungle; but if those who know this do so, they pass from one day to another as from one stream to another and from one safe place to another and obtain well-being in the world of heaven."[2]

Thus while the Upanishads are regarded as the quintessence of the honey which has been gathered from the flowers of the

[1] Brihadaranyaka Upanishad I. iv. 10. (S.B.E. XV, 88.)
[2] Satapatha Brahmana (Tr. Eggeling). Pt. V. (XII, ii. 3, 12). (S. B. E. XLIV, 160.)

sacrifice by the unceasing activity of the Brahmans and stored up in the honeycomb of the Vedas, they are nevertheless *Vedanta*—the end of the Vedas—in an equivocal sense, since the discovery of metaphysical intuition and the transcendent experience of identity mean that the whole ceremonial order and the law of works have been transcended and overcome.

The external sacrifice is good: it brings a man wealth, long life and offspring. It even brings him to the world of the gods. But " as here on earth whatever has been acquired by exertion perishes, so perishes whatever is acquired for the next world by sacrifices and other good actions performed on earth ".[1]

" Frail in truth," says the Mundaka Upanishad, " are those boats, the sacrifices, the eighteen, in which this lower ceremonial has been told. Fools who praise this as the highest good are subject again and again to old age and death.

" Fools dwelling in darkness, within their own conceit and puffed up with vain knowledge, go round and round, staggering to and fro, like blind men led by the blind."[2]

" The lower knowledge is the Rig Veda, Yagur Veda, Sama Veda, Atharva Veda (the science of) phonetics, ritual law, grammar, etymology, metre, astronomy; but the higher knowledge is that by which the Indestructible is apprehended.

" That which cannot be seen or seized, which has no family and no caste, no eyes nor ears, no hands nor feet, the Eternal, the All Pervading, the Infinitesimal, that which is imperishable, that it is which the wise regard as the source of all beings."[3]

" Considering sacrifice and good works as the best, fools know no higher good and having enjoyed (their reward) on the height of heaven, gained by good works, they enter again this world or a lower one.

" But those who practise penance and faith in the forest,

[1] Chandogya Up. VIII, 1. 6. (S. B. E. I, 127.)
[2] Mundaka Up. I, ii. 7–8. (S. B. E. XV, 31–2.)
[3] *ibid.* I, i. 5–6. (27–8.)

tranquil, wise and living on alms, depart free from passion through the sun to where that immortal Person dwells whose nature is imperishable."[1]

" Let a Brahmin after he has examined all the worlds that are gained by works, acquire freedom from all desires. That which is uncreated is not attained by works."[2]

V

But as the law of sacrifice and ritual science are transcended, the social function of the priesthood and the whole world of culture are equally transcended. The Brahmin becomes a hermit, an ascetic who renounces the world and the life of society in order to gain enlightenment and release. And this transcendent supercultural ideal of religion which finds its first conscious expression in the Upanishads is equally or even more characteristic of the new disciplines of salvation which were founded by the Buddha and Mahavira in the sixth century B.C.

Buddhism and Jainism were the creation of non-Brahmins, who rejected the Vedas and the Vedic gods—or indeed any gods whatever. Nevertheless the Buddhist monks and the Jain ascetics are the lineal descendents of the Brahmins and their thought is a logical development of the old tradition of Indian religion. It is in fact the great achievement of India to have created a culture in which the religion of pure contemplation which deliberately transcends and denies all cultural values can flourish without destroying its own social basis. To the Buddhist the world is evil, life is suffering, everything is impermanent, unreal and soulless. Yet the Law and the Order and the Buddha abide as sure guides and refuges to whom worship and prayer is directed as to the gods in other religions.

[1] Mundaka Up. I, ii. 10–11. (32.)   [2] ibid. I, ii. 12. (XV, 32.)

Thus Buddhism is a kind of sublimated Brahminism in which the rite of sacrifice is replaced by moral asceticism, and the priestly caste by the monastic order.

At first sight it would seem that this extreme sublimation, which excludes all positive religious beliefs and satisfactions, must create an atmosphere too rarified for man to breathe. Yet, as I have already remarked, Buddhism has been one of the great missionary world religions and has influenced culture even more widely than Brahminism itself.

It is true that in the course of this expansion it has re-acquired many of the elements in the priestly tradition that it had originally rejected, even down to the crude and obscene ritual of Tantric magic. But this is only one side of the development; elsewhere the sublimated ethics of the primitive doctrine has been preserved intact and the yellow-robed monks of the primitive observance still maintain the precepts of the original community.

Buddhism throughout the ages has in fact been a standing proof that the total denial of the value of culture does not prevent a religion from having an influence on culture. This is due above all to the strength of the institutional element in Buddhism: and especially to the great central institution of the monastic order, which is at once an organ for the diffusion of religious culture and the guardian of a learned tradition. In the sphere of literary culture, in particular, Buddhist monasticism exerted an enormous influence throughout Central Asia and the Far East by its tireless activity in the translation and diffusion of a great range of theological, metaphysical and literary works. This literature forms the background of all the vernacular literatures of the East from Mongolia and Tibet to Korea and Ceylon, and even in China it has had a profound influence on the thought of the second great civilization of Eastern Asia.

And in addition to these surviving civilizations, there is the great extinct culture of Eastern Turkestan with its forgotten Indo-European languages and its great Indo-Iranian art which represents the fusion of Indian, Iranian and Chinese elements under Buddhist influence.

VI

In India itself, however, the tradition of culture was so deeply connected with the religion of the priesthood and the sacrifice that the latter survived and triumphed over the great secondary disciplines of salvation which were its offshoots. Indeed owing to the rise of the temple cultus and the theistic developments of Vishnuism and Sivaism which are associated with it, modern Hinduism in some respects conforms more closely to the classical type of priestly culture as developed in the Near East than the religion of the Vedic period which represents an exceptional and indeed unique development.

In Southern and Eastern India, on the other hand, in the valleys of the Cauvery, the Vaigai, the Kistna and the Mahanadi, we find all the characteristic features of the archaic culture—artificial irrigation, temple cities, such as Madura, Srirangam, Tanjore and Puri, the cult of the mother goddess, the worship of images and a whole series of related institutions closely parallel to those which existed four or five thousand years ago in Mesopotamia and Syria.

Yet this cultural complex has become thoroughly fused with the ritual tradition of the Brahmans and with the philosophic theology of the Vedanta. Indeed since the early middle ages the latter has found its most famous centres of learning and its greatest teachers in the far south, notably at Sringeri and Srirangam—the head monasteries of Sankara and Ramanuja.[1]

[1]Ramanuja (d. A.D. 1137) was the leader of the Vaishnara sect in Southern India and the classical opponent of the theistic form of Vedantic philosophy—

PRIESTHOOD AND SACRIFICE

It is true that in the course of ages the Brahmins have lost their original character of a hereditary priesthood who lived for and by the sacrifice and have become merely a privileged sacred order. Nevertheless the doctrine of the sacrifice has never disappeared and has even received its scientific formulation in an independent philosophical school, the Karma Mimamsa, which is parallel to the Vedanta and, to an even greater degree than the Vedanta itself, is the classical system of orthodox Indian religion. Here the sacrifice retains all the importance that it had in the Brahmanas. Indeed its importance is even greater, since the gods to whom the sacrifice is offered have sunk to a very secondary position. They are merely that to which sacrifice is offered and have no independent existence apart from the rite. The power of the sacrifice has nothing to do with god or gods, it is an invisible transcendent principle (*apurva*) that is generated by the sacrifice and needs no external power to make it efficacious. Thus the Karma Mimamsa in its classical form is atheistic, in the same way as early Buddhism is atheistic. But it is an atheistic ritualism that insists on the value of those elements which Buddhism has discarded. The world is real. It is an eternal process of becoming and passing away in which the soul in its unending series of lives may by the power of sacrifice become progressively purified, until it finally attains complete freedom from the body in a state of pure consciousness. Here the institutions of priesthood and sacrifice attain a degree of sublimation which is hardly inferior to that of Buddhism. In fact the Karma Mimamsa, no less than the Vedanta and the Buddhist schools, exemplifies the intellectualism of the Indian religious tradition, which has been, from beginning to end, the tradition of a learned priestly class.

Visishtadvaita—or modified monism, against the pure monism (Advaita) of Sankara. Unlike the latter, he taught that the ascetic should perform the duties of his caste and remain faithful to the Law of Works.

VII

This intellectualism is, as I suggested at the beginning of this chapter, the characteristic mark of the priestly institution which distinguishes the Priest from the other typical sacred figures—the Prophet and the King. The Prophet is the organ of divine inspiration, the King is the organ of sacred power, but the Priest is the organ of knowledge—the master of sacred science. And this is to be seen not only in advanced and highly intellectualized cultures, like that of India; it is already manifest in the higher forms of barbarian society, in Polynesia, in parts of Africa and in America. Perhaps the most complete and certainly the most fully-studied example is to be found in the Pueblo culture of New Mexico which has survived intact through all the changes of surrounding cultures, thanks to the stabilizing power of a sacred ritual maintained by the tradition of the priesthood.

In her striking studies of Zuni culture Miss Ruth Benedict has shown how the whole social life of the people is absorbed and dominated by their rich and complex ritual order.

" Their cults of the masked gods, of healing, of the sun, of the sacred fetishes, of war, of the dead," she writes, " are formal and established bodies of ritual with priestly officials and calendric observances. No field of activity competes with ritual for foremost place in their attention. Probably most grown men among the Western Pueblos give to it the greater part of their working life. It requires the memorizing of an amount of word-perfect ritual which our less trained minds find staggering, and the performance of neatly dovetailed ceremonies that are charted by the calendar and complexly interlock all the different cults and the governing body in endless formal procedure."[1]

In such a society the priest is inevitably the leading figure, and he owes his power and prestige not to his individual

[1] R. Benedict. *Patterns of Culture*, pp. 59–60.

inspiration or character but to his knowledge and his initiation into an inherited tradition of ritual science. " The Zuni phrase for a person with power is ' one who knows how ' ",[1] and the priest is the man " who knows how " in the sacred techniques which govern the relations of the community with the transcendent powers.

It is true that these techniques are not essentially different from those to be found amongst the most primitive peoples —masked dances, rain-making ceremonies, fertility rites and the rest. The difference lies in the higher degree of integration that they have attained, with the result that Zuni society achieves the ideal of a liturgical culture in which the whole corporate way of life is ordered to the service of the gods in a continual cycle of prayer and sacramental action.

And it is the same with the institution of priesthood itself. Looked at from one side, the Zuni priest is indistinguishable from the savage magician or medicine-man. But looked at from the other, he is obviously closely akin to the temple priesthoods of Central America, which in turn are identical in social function and intellectual position with the great temple priesthoods of the archaic culture in Mesopotamia and Egypt.

VIII

Now as it is possible to trace the connection between the magician and the priest in the lower cultures, so in the higher we can see the relation between the priest and the man of learning. In our own Western culture above all, the historic origins of the intelligentsia—the professional learned class or the intellectual élite—are to be found in the clergy, the mediaeval priesthood with its subordinate orders of clerks, together with the religious orders. It was the clergy that

[1] R. Benedict. *Patterns of Culture*, p. 96.

created the European university and controlled the whole educational system. In Europe, no less than in India, the sacred language was also the learned language, and the clergy possessed a quasi-monopoly of the higher intellectual culture.

And though humanism marked the beginning of the secularization of this tradition, humanism itself remained closely associated with the pre-existing clerical culture. The universities remained clerical corporations down to the end of the seventeenth century and in England until much later.

The representatives of this tradition have not only been the intellectual guides of their own culture and guardians of its norms; they have also tended to be the chief interpreters and intermediaries between different cultures.

As a rule the relations between cultures are apt to be dominated by aggressive motives and attitudes. To the common man, the member of a different culture, even more than the member of another race, is a " barbarian ", " an infidel ", a " foreign devil ", while the conquerors, the prospectors and the traders inevitably tend to limit their intercourse to the more superficial and external aspects of social life. It is only when the religions of different cultures come into touch with one another, either by syncretism or by missionary activity, that real contact is made with the spirit of the alien culture.

And it is the priesthood that has been the traditional agent of such contacts from the time of Berosus and Manetho[1] to the Jesuit scholars in China and modern missionaries like W. W. Gill who salvaged so much of the cultural traditions of Mangaia before they were finally lost.[2]

[1] Berosus, the high priest of the great temple of Bel at Babylon, wrote the standard Greek history of Babylonia and dedicated it to Antiochus I. Manetho, also a priest, composed a similar work on Egyptian history for Ptolemy II. Although both these histories have been lost, their lists of the dynasties which were preserved formed the backbone of ancient history down to the discoveries of modern archaeology and still possess some importance.
[2] Of Mangaia, a small island in the Cook Group, H. M. and N. K.

This is contrary to the commonly accepted view that a priesthood is always the focus of cultural intolerance and that the missionaries are primarily responsible for the destruction of primitive cultures. But though there is an element of truth in this view, the destruction of a conquered culture has been most complete when it has been due to purely secular motives, while even the most rigid and exclusive orthodoxy is not inconsistent with an intelligent interest in the beliefs and institutions of potential converts, as we can see, for example, in the elaborate and systematic attempt of the Franciscan missionary Bernard de Sahagun to produce an authenticated record of the religious beliefs of the Mexicans in the early days of the Conquest.

And on the other side, from the standpoint of the conquered people, we have men like Rammohun Roy the Bengal Brahmin and religious reformer, who did more to bridge the gulf between European and Indian culture than any other man of his generation, or Iswar Chandra Vidyasagar (1820–1891) who carried on a similar work in the following generation.

In these and countless other instances the priesthood has fulfilled a cultural as well as a religious function, and this duality of function is rooted in the nature of the institution, since from the beginning the priest has been a teacher as well as one who offers sacrifice. The tradition of a learned priesthood lies at the heart of all the great civilizations of the world except China and Hellas, and even when a culture has been secularized the tradition is still not altogether lost, as we see in the case of men like Matthew Arnold and Emerson who not only regarded themselves as priests of culture, but were in fact the social products of an hereditary priestly tradition.

Chadwick write: " It was for many centuries probably the most literary community of its size in the world." *The Growth of Literature*, III, 232. Mr. Gill owed his information chiefly to Tereavai, the last priest of the shark god, Tiaio, and afterwards a deacon of the London Missionary Society.

It is, however, questionable whether a culture which has once possessed an institution of this nature—I mean a spiritual class or order that has been the guardian of a sacred tradition of culture—can dispense with it without becoming impoverished and disorientated. This is what has actually occurred in the secularization of modern Western culture, and men have been more or less aware of it ever since the beginning of the last century. In particular it was recognized with great acuteness by Auguste Comte who in his theory of society stressed the distinction between the temporal and spiritual powers and insisted on the necessity of finding appropriate organs for them at every stage of culture. The solution that he offered in his Religion of Humanity proved completely ineffective, as must always be the case when an artificial intellectual construction is offered as the satisfaction of a real religious need. But from the sociological point of view his analysis is perfectly sound, and the existence of some social embodiment of the higher spiritual principle in culture remains one of the fundamental conditions of an enduring social order.

The fact that the intelligentsia in modern Europe no longer possesses this spiritual principle is one of the main causes of the instability and restlessness of contemporary society, and it has produced the accusations of the *trahison des clercs* which have been so often heard in recent years. For the intellectuals who have succeeded the priests as the guardians of the higher tradition of Western culture have been strong only in their negative work of criticism and disintegration. They have failed to provide an integrated system of principles and values which could unify modern society, and consequently they have proved unable to resist the non-moral, inhuman and irrational forces which are destroying the humanist no less than the Christian traditions of Western culture.

The Sources of Religious Knowledge and the Religious Organs of Society

(III) Kingship

IMPORTANCE of the religious functions of kingship in ancient society. The embodiment of sacred power in a representative person. Mana and the divine right of kings. The myth of divine origins. Kingship and the diffusion of culture. Kingship and the origins of the archaic culture in the Near East. The tradition of the Divine Kingship in Egypt. The king and the cult of the dead. The king and the worship of the Sun God. The apotheosis of the dead king and the dogma of royal immortality. The moral responsibility of kingship. The Egyptian goddess of justice. Egyptian association of justice with the divine king, on the one hand, and with the last judgment of the soul, on the other. Universalist tendencies in Egyptian theocratic monarchy. The religious reformation of Ikhnaton in the fourteenth century B.C. Parallels to Egyptian sacred kingship in modern African cultures. Persistence of the tradition of sacred monarchy in the higher cultures.

The Sources of Religious Knowledge and the Religious Organs of Society

(III) KINGSHIP

I

IF THE Priesthood is the classical type of a social organ which is created for specifically religious ends, Kingship is the type of an institution which exists for a distinctively political function but which owes its social prestige to its religious or divine character. From the beginning of history the king has been distinguished from the tyrant, the magistrate or the official by the possession of a *charisma* or divine mandate which sets him apart from other men; so that even to-day the crown and sceptre which are the symbols of this sacred character remain the emblem of royalty as they were 5,000 years ago. No doubt these things to-day have a vestigial and antiquarian character and no longer represent living forces in either the political or the religious sphere. But they could not have survived in the alien atmosphere of modern times had they not been exceptionally deeply rooted in the tradition of culture, and the deeper we delve into the origins of our civilization and of every civilization, the larger is the place that kingship holds in both the religious and the social pattern of life and thought.

Now we have seen how great an importance the idea of transcendent or supernatural power possesses in primitive religion. But this belief does not seem to have been originally associated with the earliest forms of political power. The old idea that primitive society was ruled despotically by the power of the Stronger—an idea which appears in mediaeval literature and still lingers in the Freudian theory of the primitive ape-like human horde—is not borne out by the ethnological evidence. On the contrary, it seems that the simplest and the most primitive types of society such as we see in the Arctic, in Australia and among the Pigmies and the Bushmen are democratic or gerontocratic, while the absolute power of the warrior chieftain, which made such a deep impression on the first European travellers in West Africa, Uganda, Zululand and Rhodesia, was the product of a relatively advanced type of social organization. The consecration of power in a formal institution does not take place until the ground has been prepared by a process of social differentiation.

On the other hand, the idea that what we call the " gift of leadership " has a supernatural quality or origin akin to the gift of prophecy and divination is a very primitive one. We see this idea in its simplest form in the Biblical story of Samson— the strong man, the champion of his oppressed people, on whom the spirit of Jehovah suddenly descends so that he smites the Philistines single-handed (Judges xiv. 6, xv. 14–16). This superhuman power which manifests itself in a sudden outburst of energy or in some incalculable decisive act is so remote from our own religious traditions that it is very difficult for us to realize its religious character. Among modern writers Goethe stands almost alone in his sympathetic understanding of it, and though he is concerned primarily with its manifestation in the form of poetic genius, his analysis of its nature in *Dichtung und Wahrheit* is even more illuminating when it is applied to primitive religion.

" It was," he writes, " something that only manifested itself in contradictions and therefore could not be comprehended under any concept, still less under any one word. It was not divine, for it seemed unreasonable; not human, for it lacked understanding; not angelic, for it often displayed malicious joy. It was like chance, for it pointed to no consequence; it resembled providence, for it indicated connexion and unity. All that hems us in seemed penetrable to it; it seemed to dispose at will of the inevitable elements of our being, contracting time and expanding space. Only in the impossible did it seem at home and the possible it spurned from itself with contempt.

" Although this daimonic thing can be manifested in everything corporeal and incorporeal, finding indeed most notable expression among animals; still it is pre-eminently with men that it stands in closest and most marvellous connection, and there fashions a power which if not opposed to the moral world order, yet intersects it in such a way that the one might be taken for the warp and the other for the woof."

And he concludes, " This daimonic character appears in its most dreadful form when it stands out dominatingly in some *Man*. Such are not always the most remarkable men either in spiritual quality or natural talents and they seldom have any goodness of heart to recommend them. But an incredible force goes forth from them and they exercise an incredible power over all creatures, nay perhaps even over the elements. And who can say how far such an influence may not extend? "[1]

Goethe's mind seems to have been much preoccupied with this idea at a certain period: we find him returning to it again in one of the most striking of the conversations reported by Eckermann in which he refers to Napoleon as a type of the daimonic man.

It is unnecessary to point out what dangerous possibilities are involved in this concept so far as modern political life is concerned. On the other hand, it is of great value and importance

[1] *Dichtung und Wahrheit*. (Werke, ed. Cotta XXV), pp. 124, 126.

as a key to the understanding of primitive thought. For it is in this sense of the daimonic that we find the psychological root of King worship and of the Divine Kingship. And here I must record my disagreement with the thesis of the late Professor Hocart who has contributed so much to our understanding of the ritual pattern of the institution of kingship. For Hocart always tends to minimize the religious elements in the institution and to explain its origin and importance on natural utilitarian grounds. " We have seen reason to think," he writes, for example, " that the original priest king was not a person of great majesty; prosaic, at times grotesque, his humdrum function was to ensure a regular supply of food and a satisfactory birthrate by the best means inference could suggest, whether dignified or undignified."

Now it seems to me that this line of interpretation, which is characteristic of a large school of anthropologists, is radically mistaken, since it reverses the real sequence of primitive thought. The modern tends to oppose the useful to the religious and to apply the criterion of secular utilitarianism to customs and institutions of a totally different order.

But to the primitive this opposition does not exist: the sacred is socially useful and what is socially useful is generally related to what is religiously valuable. Consequently the religious importance of kingship is not due to the practical social advantages that it confers but to the more irrational psychological attitude of wonder and terror which is diagnosed so well by Goethe in the passages which I have just quoted.

II

For primitive man is quick to recognize this inexplicable overpowering quality; not only in prophecy and inspiration, but in heroism and in wise counsel, and where he finds it he recognizes it as divine. It is the *mana* of the chief, to use the Polynesian term, which contains something of the sense of grace, and good fortune and supernatural power and divine right, and what our heathen ancestors called " the luck of the king ".

But before the social implications of this concept could be fully developed, the personal gifts of the leader must be reinforced by a further element of hereditary sanctity, which is most strongly marked in the Polynesian concept of *mana* itself. It is not enough for a chief to possess personal prowess and prestige, he must inherit his sacred authority from sacred ancestors: he must be of the blood royal and of divine origin. Hence in spite of the material poverty of a culture which knew neither the potter's wheel, nor the smith's hammer, nor the weaver's loom, the Polynesian was as skilled and learned in genealogy as a mediaeval herald. It is recorded on good authority that a Maori chief once established the claims of his clan before the Land Commission at Ruatoki with a pedigree of thirty-four generations which took three days to recite and contained over 1,400 names.[1]

This preoccupation with blood and lineage and this belief in the divine origin of kings—the sons of God who took wives of the daughters of men—is almost universal among peoples who have advanced beyond the most primitive stages of culture. We find it among the Polynesians and the Melanesians, among the Indians and the Greeks, among our own Celtic and Teutonic ancestors and among the Egyptians and the other peoples of the ancient East. It is often associated with a legend of cultural origins, so that the divine kings are also heroes and culture bearers who come from some divine homeland—like the mythical Hawaiki of the Polynesians. It is easy enough to understand this, since every migration involves a process of

[1] Elsdon Best. *The Maori School of Learning*, p. 5. (1923.)

culture diffusion, and the resultant mingling of peoples and races accentuates the value and prestige of the stronger element. In modern times we have the authentic case of the identification of Captain Cook with the great god Rongo or Lono in Hawaii, and his coming is also commemorated in the literature of other far distant regions of the Pacific, so that had it been an isolated episode and not the starting point of European occupation, it might well have become incorporated in Polynesian mythology.

Mythology and history alike bear witness to the religious and sociological importance of events of this kind. We have, for example, the story of Quetzalcoatl in Central America, the legend of the foundation of the Inca monarchy in Peru, and the foundation of the Bahima monarchies in Central Africa. There seems, indeed, reason to believe that the institution of sacred kingship is linked with the diffusion of culture and had its origins in the centres of the archaic culture from which this movement of diffusion started.

This does not however justify the Pan-Egyptian theory of the late Professor Elliot Smith and Dr. Perry which postulates a single vast movement of culture diffusion by which every element of the higher culture is ultimately derived from the archaic culture of Egypt with its divine monarchy and its solar religion. On the contrary, the process of culture diffusion is highly complex and multi-linear, and every centre of the archaic culture had its own social and religious institutions and acted as an independent source of cultural influence and diffusion. We still know too little of the great revolutionary change in human life which occurred in Western Asia and Egypt from the sixth to the fourth millenium B.C. and on which all the subsequent achievements of the higher culture are based. Modern discoveries in Mesopotamia and Syria and Palestine have however revealed a series of cultures based on irrigation and cattle breeding with a well developed religious cult in the periods known as the Halafian and Ghassulian, after the sites at Tell Halaf in Northern Mesopotamia and at Telleilat el Ghassul near Jericho. Finally by the fourth millennium the artificial control of the flood waters of the great river-valleys and deltas of Babylonia and Egypt by the construction of canals and the draining of the marshes prepared the way for the rise of the historic civilization of ancient Sumer and the Old Kingdom of Egypt.

III

This creative movement which gave birth to the archaic civilization is dominated by the figure of the Sacred King. It was the age of " the Dead Demi-gods ", the Followers of Horus who united the Two Lands, in Egypt, and of the legendary kings who founded the first city states of Sumer like Gilgamesh who built the great wall at Erech and founded the temple of Ea Anna.

It is clear that this concentration of religious and social power was directly connected with the revolutionary changes in man's way of life represented by the rise of the archaic culture. The discovery of irrigation and intensive agriculture not only made possible a great advance in population, wealth and social organization, it altered man's whole outlook on the world. The divine powers on which human life depended were no longer alien and incalculable forces, like the gods of the hunters: they had initiated man into their mysteries, teaching him the way of life and co-operating with him to increase the fruits of the earth a hundredfold. And since this socialization of religion went hand in hand with the concentration of social power, it was inevitable that the king, who was the figure in whom the whole process culminated, should be regarded not merely as sacred but as himself a divine power, a god or a son of the gods, at once god and man, priest and king, the keystone which joined the arch of heaven and earth and established the harmony of the two worlds.

This is the archetypal pattern of the archaic culture which underlies all the most ancient civilizations of the world.

IV

But it is in Egypt that we see it most clearly and most completely, since it was there that the conditions for the concentration of power were most completely fulfilled. The Nile valley, united and irrigated by the river and segregated and defended by the desert, was more self-contained and more adapted to centralized control than the lands of the other great riverine civilizations of the Ancient East, and when once it had been united by the rulers of the First Dynasty, the tradition of unity was never destroyed.

Hence it was natural that the person of the king who embodied this unity and on whose power and wisdom the welfare of the whole of Egypt depended should also be regarded as the embodiment of the divine powers which ruled the life of the land. It is possible that this idea goes back to predynastic times and that in each of the Nomes the head of the community was regarded as the representative and embodiment of the local divinity, which was usually represented in the form of an animal, bird or plant. The unification of Egypt seems therefore to have been accompanied by a process of syncretism by which the king accumulated a series of sacred prerogatives and was identified or closely associated with a number of different divine figures. Thus apart from Horus, the divine falcon of Edfu, who was the royal god *par excellence*, there were the two guardians of the crowns of Upper and Lower Egypt, the vulture goddess of Nekheb, and the serpent of

Buto; while on a higher, more universal plane the king became associated with Re, the sun-god of Heliopolis, and with Osiris, the vegetation god of Abu Sir, the lord of the underworld and the king of the dead.

Out of these diverse elements there arose an immensely powerful complex of mythology and symbolism which surrounded the person of the king with an aura of sanctity and divinity more impressive than anything to be found in the other centres of archaic culture.

This was due in the first place to the precocious concentration of power which characterized the Egyptian development. The king was not merely the representative of his people. He was Egypt and Egypt existed only in and by and for him. From the earliest times his is the only figure which appears in art in the presence of the gods. It is the king, and not the priest, who is shown offering the sacrifice. It is the king, and not the army, who smites the enemy in the presence of the gods. It is the king, and not the peasant, who provides food and nourishment for men and gods and who controls and directs the waters of the inundation.

" *How great is the Lord towards his City. He alone is millions, other men are but small.*

He has come to us: he has seized Upper Egypt and placed the White Crown upon his head.

He has united the two countries and joined the Reed [the symbol of Upper Egypt] with the Bee [the symbol of the Delta].

He has conquered the Black Land [the Nile Valley] and has subjected the Red [the desert].

He has protected the Two Lands and given peace to the two banks.

He has given life to Egypt, and abolished her sufferings.

He has given life to men, and made the throat of the dead to breathe.

He has trodden down the strangers and smitten the Troglodytes that feared him not.

He has fought for his frontier and driven back the spoilers.

He has granted us to rear our children and to bury our aged [in peace].[1]

But from the theological point of view Pharaoh owed his unique character to the fusion of the two mythologies of Re and Osiris in both of which he held a central position. A mystical correspondence was established between the dying and reviving Osiris, the god of vegetation and of the rising and falling waters of the Nile, the King of the Underworld and the Judge of the Dead, and the rising and setting sun which sailed in the divine bark from the eastern to the western horizon and returned nightly on the subterranean waters of the second Nile that flows through the realm of Osiris. And in the same way there is a mysterious correspondence between the dead king reigning in his tomb and his son, the living Horus, who " rises " on his throne bearing the great double crown of Upper and Lower Egypt like the sun ascending the vault of heaven.

This double deification of the ruler gave rise not only to the elaborate mortuary ritual of the royal tombs in which the mummy of Pharaoh is surrounded with all the requisites for his life in the underworld, as we find also in the royal tombs of Ur; but further to the conception of a heavenly kingdom, an ascent to the world of the Sun-god which is the earliest known vision of a celestial hereafter. The Pyramid Texts, which are the earliest religious documents that we possess, are all dominated by a tremendous assertion of the dogma of royal immortality. " Rise up, rise up, King Pepi, thou diest not. Have ye said

[1] Erman, *Literatur der Aegypter*, pp. 179–82.

that he would die? He dies not. This King Pepi lives for ever-more." " Opened are the two doors of the horizon, its bolts are drawn back. O men and gods your arms under King Pepi! Raise him up, lift him to the heaven, as the arms of the air god Shu are under the heaven and he raises it. To the heavens, to the heavens! to the great seat among the gods! "[1]

The Pyramid Texts are full of passages which describe the life of the glorified Pharaoh in heaven, dwelling as a god with the gods, sailing with Re in his divine sky boat, sharing the divine offerings and eating the fruit of the Tree of Life.

" This King Pepi opened his path like the fowlers, he exchanged greetings with the lords of the souls, he went to the great isle in the midst of the Field of Offering over which the gods make the swallows fly. The swallows are the imperishable stars. They give to this King Pepi this tree of life whereof they live that you [the King and the Morning Star] may at the same time live thereof."[2]

This divine apotheosis of the dead king endures throughout Egyptian history, but it reached its climax at a relatively early date with the great pyramid builders of the Fourth Dynasty when the whole resources of the first centralized state in history were concentrated on the erection of these vast sepulchral monuments.

It is easy to see how the development of the cult of the Sun-god and that of the divine monarchy mutually supported one another, so that the Sun-god became more of a celestial monarch and the monarch more of a god. But it is more difficult to estimate the loss and gain that it represented both for religion and for culture.

On the one hand, the immense gulf that it created between the person of the ruler and the subject population increased the

[1] Tr. J. H. Breasted, *The Dawn of Conscience*, p. 79 (1933).
[2] Tr. J. H. Breasted, *The Dawn of Conscience*, p. 92.

possibilities of injustice and oppression, so that, as whenever the absolute state acquires a religious sanction, it imposed an unbearable material burden on human nature and on the life of the people.

It may be that the memory of this survived in the legends of a younger world about the impiety and oppression of the great pyramid builders which Herodotus records. Yet there is much to be said on the other side, since it is clear that these colossal works were not due to the whim of an arbitrary despot but were an act of faith of a whole people. Moreover it is in connection with the solar religion, the solar monarchy, and the celestial hereafter, that we find the first clear conception of a law of justice which is at once social and divine.

Maat—Justice—is the first abstract divinity and she is both the daughter of the Sun-god and the power which inspires and gives validity to the king's command. And since the king himself on entering the celestial kingdom had to face the judgment of Re and justify himself before the divine tribunal, the idea of Justice acquired a transcendent character. Already in the *Instruction of Ptahhotep*, the earliest relic of Egyptian literature, the wise man says " Great is Maat; its dispensation endures nor has it been overthrown from the time of its creation."[1] And in the age of disorder that followed the fall of the Old Kingdom, we find a clear recognition of the responsibility of earthly power before the judgment of heaven.

Thus King Merikere repeats the teaching he has received from his father that he who acts unjustly must give account of his actions before a higher tribunal. " The divine judges who judge the unworthy, thou knowest that they are not lenient in the day of judgment. Woe to thee if the accuser is the Wise One (Thoth). Trust not in the length of years, for they behold life in a moment. A man survives after his passing over and

[1] Tr. J. H. Breasted, *The Dawn of Conscience*, p. 148.

his deeds are piled up like mountains. For it is eternity which awaits man there and a fool is he who despises it. But he who comes there without having committed sin, he shall live like a god, going onward freely like the lords of eternity."[1]

So too in the speech of the Eloquent Peasant, which was perhaps the best known work of this early literature, " Do justice for the Lord of Justice. . . . For justice is for eternity. It descends with him that does justice into the grave, when he is placed in the coffin and laid in the earth. His name is not effaced on earth but he is remembered because of justice. Such is the uprightness of the word of God, which is as a true balance which weigheth not falsely."[2]

This association of justice with kingship, on the one hand, and with the justification of the immortal soul before the divine tribunal, on the other, became an essential element of Egyptian religion. After the fusion of the Osirian and the solar mythologies was completed, the judgment after death was no longer confined to the king and his family and court, but was regarded as the destiny of every man, who had to give an account of his deeds in the Hall of Justice in the presence of Osiris. By degrees the common man came to share in the privileges and moral responsibilities attached to the celestial immortality of the divine king. Thus the way was opened for a new form of personal religion and personal piety, which in spite of grotesque magical elements also shows remarkably high moral ideals, as for example in the so-called " Negative Confession " of the Book of the Dead.

V

But this popularization of the religion of immortality and the cult of Osiris did not involve any diminution of the religious

---

[1] *The Instruction of Merikere*, 12–13.
[2] Tr. J. H. Breasted, *The Dawn of Conscience*, p. 191.

importance of the monarchy. On the contrary it was at this period from the sixteenth to the thirteenth centuries B.C. that the kings of the New Empire brought the solar cult to its full development as a universal and quasi-monotheistic imperial religion. The most striking expression of this was the attempt to create a new state religion by Ikhnaton, which may almost be regarded as the first conscious experiment in natural theology. It shows in a remarkable way how, even in a most rigidly hierarchical culture, the theocratic monarchy may itself become the agent of revolutionary religious change.

Under the great Pharaohs of the eighteenth dynasty Egypt had become a world power with an Asiatic empire and international relations with the distant kingdoms of Asia Minor and Mesopotamia, and the universalism of the new religion corresponded to the cosmopolitanism of the new imperial culture.

The traditional mythology of the Egyptian pantheon was drastically swept aside and replaced by the one universal solar divinity (always represented in the form of the Sun Disk—the Aton) and by his one earthly representative the Sun King—Ikhnaton.

" How numerous are thy works, that which thou hast created and that which is hidden O thou only god who hast no equal. Thou hast created the earth according to thy heart, thou alone, even men and beasts, all that is on the earth and goes on foot, all that is in the air and flies on wings, all foreign lands, Syria and Nubia and the land of Egypt.

" Thou makest millions of forms through thyself alone; homes and cities and villages, highways and rivers: all eyes see thee before them, the disk of day over the earth. Thou art in my heart. There is no other who knoweth thee save me thy son Ikhnaton. Thou hast made him wise in thy ways and in thy power."[1]

[1] Tr. J. H. Breasted, *The Dawn of Conscience*, pp. 281–6.

The spirit which inspires this great hymn finds its artistic expression in the naturalism and humanism of the royal art of Tell el Amarna the Aton city, which shows the transforming influence of the new religious ideas on the traditional styles and motifs of Egyptian painting and sculpture. But for all that, the history of Ikhnaton and the new solar monotheism is not only an instance of the transforming power of kingship in religion and culture, it also shows its limitations. For the whole episode was a transitory phase in the history of Egyptian religion, and a few years after the death of Ikhnaton the old gods and the old mythology reappear to survive unchanged down to Hellenistic and Roman times.

The tendency to universalism did not, however, disappear and shows itself hardly less strongly in the great Theban hymn to the Sun-god, as creator and universal ruler, than in the religion of the Aton itself.

VI

The influence of the Egyptian sacred monarchy was not confined to the highly specialized environment in which it developed but affected all the neighbouring cultures of the Near East. It is seen most clearly to the south in the daughter culture of Nubia and Nilotic Ethiopia, where a barbaric imitation of the Egyptian monarchy dominated the Upper Nile and the Eastern Sudan for more than a thousand years. It is difficult to over-estimate the importance of this secondary culture centre in the history of African culture, but on the other hand it is equally difficult to distinguish between those cultural institutions and religious ideas that are derived from Egyptian origins and those which are the result of a parallel development deriving from a common origin in prehistoric times.

Thus the institution of kingship is strongly developed among the primitive Nilotic tribes of the Bahr el Ghazel, while far to the west in Nigeria we find a number of states which preserve the tradition of sacred monarchy in an exceptionally complete and highly developed form.

Here we have examples of divine kings and priest kings, whose existence was hedged round by a network of ritual prescriptions and sacred tabus, since their life was the life of the land, and the river and the harvest depended on their well-being. Thus among the Jukun of Central Nigeria, according to Dr. Meek, the death of a king was never openly admitted since this would destroy the harvest: " it would be an invitation to the crops to wither up."

This Osirian identification of the king with the life of the earth is shown very clearly in the words addressed to a new king on his investiture with the royal robes, the whip and the seed corn. " To-day," they say, " we have given you the house of your father. The whole world is yours. You are our guinea corn and beans, our *jô* and our *aku* (i.e. the spirits and gods of our worship). Henceforth we have no father and mother. But you are the father and mother of all. Follow in the footsteps of your forefathers and do evil to no one, that your people may abide with you and that we may come to the end of your reign in peace."[1]

It is interesting to note that according to Dr. Meek this sacred king was not a war king. He did not lead his army in the field. Only when the city was attacked and the people was in dire necessity he would appear among the warriors shrouded from head to foot and bearing the sacred spear.

The Jukun are a dying people—an interesting but effete survival from the vanished past. But four hundred miles to

[1] Meek, *Jukun—A Sudanese Kingdom*, 1931, p. 137. See also *Pagan Tribes of the Nilotic Sudan*, C. G. Seligman, p. 40.

the west we can see equally striking types of sacred kingship still flourishing among one of the most vigorous and enterprising peoples of West Africa.

The Yoruba of Oyo and the neighbouring provinces of Southern Nigeria are the most urbanized and civilized of all negro peoples. But in spite of the receptiveness they have shown towards Christianity and European influence, they have preserved almost intact their national traditions and institutions which recall to a striking degree those of the archaic culture. The Yoruba states—Oyo, Ife, Abeokuta, Ibadan, etc. —are city states ruled by sacred kings, each with his court and an elaborate official hierarchy. Ibadan is the largest negro city in Africa with a population of 387,000, but it is inferior in sanctity and prestige to Ife, the sacred city of the god of divination, Ifa, which is the religious metropolis of Yorubaland, with its 201 temples and shrines, each with its priesthood and annual festival. Here even in our own days the Oni or priest-king has been known to object to the abolition of certain sacrifices on the ground that they were necessary not merely for Ife but for the world and that their interruption might have a disastrous effect on the universal course of nature![1]

No doubt this is an extreme case of cultural survival and the general trend of social evolution or revolution in Africa and Asia as well as in Europe has been unfavourable to theocratic institutions. Nevertheless this is a very recent development, and down to the nineteenth century or even later the institution of kingship retained its religious character in varying degrees throughout the greater part of the world. It is still too early to say whether this change is permanent. It is not impossible that a century hence the people of Ife may regard the atomic bomb not as an evidence of scientific progress but

---

[1] H. Ward Price: *Land Tenure in the Yoruba Province*, p. 4 (1933). cf. M. Perham: *Native Administration in Nigeria*, p. 175 (1937).

as an unfortunate by-product of the abandonment of the theocratic order and the neglect of sacrifice.

VII

These are outstanding examples of the survival of the primitive features of the sacred monarchy which have been transmitted from people to people and from age to age by a movement of diffusion from some original centre of the archaic culture. But the examples to which I have referred in modern African society are but the backwaters and shallows of the tradition of sacred kingship; the main stream flows broad and deep through the whole course of ancient history and has had an inestimable influence on the religious life of mankind. For the adoration of transcendent power embodied in a human person and in social institutions is morally ambivalent and is associated with all that is highest and lowest in human nature. On the one hand it has led to monstrous and inhuman developments like the wholesale human sacrifices of the Great Customs of Benin and the deification of tyrants and madmen like Caligula and Al Hakim.[1] But on the other hand it has inspired the hope of a kingdom of righteousness and the advent of a divine Saviour.

And in the Old Testament we see these two developments consciously brought into relation as two rival kingdoms: on the one hand the daemonic exaltation of power viewed as the self-exaltation of man against God; and on the other, the assertion of the Kingdom of Jahweh among the Gentiles and the

---

[1] Al Hakim, the sixth Fatimid Khalif, ruled Egypt and North Africa from A.D. 996–1021. He destroyed the Church of the Holy Sepulchre in 1009, and proclaimed his own divinity. He is still regarded as divine by the Druses of Lebanon.

deliverance of the people of God by a Messianic saviour king.

And it is a remarkable thing that though nothing could be more drastic than the rejection of the divine character of the gods of the Gentiles, there is no similar denial of the sacred character of the Gentile kingship. Nowhere in literature do we find a more vivid picture of the archetypal figure of the divine priest king than in Ezekiel's description of the king of Tyre, the high priest of Melcarth, " Thou sealest up the sum, full of wisdom and perfect in beauty ". " And I set thee so that thou wast upon the holy mountain of God, thou hast walked up and down in the midst of the stones of fire. Thou wast perfect in thy ways from the day that thou wast created, until unrighteousness was found in thee." . . . " Thy heart was lifted up because of thy beauty, thou hast corrupted thy wisdom by reason of thy brightness." " Therefore have I cast thee as profane out of the mountain of God and I have destroyed thee, O covering cherub, from the midst of the stones of fire." (Ezek. XXVIII.) Here the principle is the same as that which inspired the doctrine of sacred kingship in ancient China. The king rules by the mandate of Heaven so long as he recognizes his relation of dependence. But as soon as he becomes self-assertive and transgresses the laws of Heaven, the mandate is withdrawn and the kingdom passes from him to another.

But the most remarkable expression of the idea of the divine mandate to the king by the grace of God is the great series of prophecies in Isaiah XL to LV, dealing with the divine mission of Cyrus, in which the world monarch of the coming Persian empire is announced as the chosen servant of the true God whom he does not know, anointed and set apart to realize the divine purpose of Jahweh towards His people and to the world.

This is a striking example of the way in which religious revelation in the strict theological sense can take into itself and inform with new meaning the old archetypes and institutional patterns of culture and natural religion. Nor does the process stop at this point, for the figure of Cyrus in Deutero-Isaiah becomes fused with that of the Prophet to form the archetype of a new Messianic figure.

The Divine Order and the Order of Nature. Sacred Science

How FAR is culture dependent on the processes of economic production? Spiritual creativity of culture even under primitive conditions, *e.g.*, Magdalenian art. Magical techniques for the control of nature. Frazer's theory of magic as primitive pseudo-science. Religious elements in magic. Magic and mystery. Knowledge and initiation. The three elements of religious cult—rite, myth and magical power. Connection between primitive fertility magic and the cult of the Mother Goddess and the Vegetation God in the archaic culture of the Near East. The farmer's year and the ritual cycle. The religious importance of the science of the calendar and the co-ordination of the three cycles of heaven, earth and human life. Development of the religio-philosophic concept of a universal principle of cosmic order: Rita, Tao, etc. Influence of astral theology on rational cosmology. The beginnings of science and philosophy in the attempt to explain the nature of the unity of the cosmic process which was already implicit in the religious doctrine of the sacred order. Philosophers and prophets.

The Divine Order and the Order of Nature. Sacred Science

I

EVERY human culture is a conscious adaptation of social life to man's external environment and to the order of nature. What the animal does instinctively, man does with conscious purpose and with a greater or less degree of rational calculation. Thus culture is rooted in nature, just as the higher achievements of the individual human mind are rooted in culture.

This is the basis of the Marxian theory of society and of the materialist interpretation of history. Marx argued that man must be able to subsist in order to create history and that the first and indispensable condition of life is economic production. Therefore " the mode of production in material life determines the social, political and intellectual life process in general." Reduced to its primary elements, culture is therefore nothing but the social elaboration of the process of economic production. Man builds a simple or complex hive which is at once a production unit and a social organism. The more elaborate the process of production, the more complex the organism and the more advanced the culture.

Now there is an obvious element of truth in this theory, namely, the natural material basis of all human life and action. Its materialistic bias is due to its over-simplification of the economic motive. For primitive man is not necessarily a

131

producer in the Marxian sense. The Bushman or the aboriginal Tasmanian is hardly more a producer of food than are the animals on which he preys. He differs from the animals not because he produces food but because he thinks and plans.

Religion and art are older than agriculture and industry. In the beginning was the word, and man was a seer and an artist before he was a producer. This was shown most strikingly in the later nineteenth century when a chance discovery by a little girl in a Spanish cavern revealed the existence of a great European art dating from remote prehistoric times. Living under Arctic conditions with the barest and most rudimentary material culture, man had nevertheless mastered the arts of sculpture and painting so that we can see to-day, as it were with his eyes, the living images of creatures, such as the mammoth and the woolly rhinoceros and the cave lion, which had ceased to exist before the dawn of civilization.

Thus while it is true that economic production is the necessary condition of material civilization and that the type of production affects the type of civilization by its influence on the form of society, this only represents one side of the culture process, since the essential characteristics of human culture already existed before man had become economically productive. In this pre-productive phase he had already achieved a high degree of cultural specialization and had attained the mastery over his environment even in the peculiarly unfavourable conditions of the glacial age. The proof of this mastery is to be seen in the art of the Aurignacian and Magdalenian periods. It shows us that man was spiritually creative before he was economically productive, and that there is no necessary relation between the economic development of a culture and its spiritual quality. And if this is the case with primitive art, it is still more likely to be true of religion.

For religion is not a sophisticated by-product of the economic process or—as Engels says of the idea of God—" the product of a tedious process of abstraction ",[1] it is rather one of the primary psychological forces behind the whole culture process from its very beginning. As I have already said, primitive culture is not only a simple economic way of life, it also involves a deliberate effort to bring human life into relation with divine reality and into subordination to divine powers. For the adaptation of man's life to his physical environment, even at the most primitive level, is always accompanied by a religious concern with the propitiation and cultus of the powers that are held to control that environment—the powers that manifest themselves in Nature.

For we must remember that the idea of Nature now accepted as the obvious background and basis of all our sensible experience is actually more abstract and more sophisticated than the idea of God. Primitive thought starts with gods and things and events, not with Nature and Mind or Nature and Spirit.

No doubt the whole theory of primitive magic as presented by Frazer and his school presupposes a highly rationalized and quasi-scientific attitude to nature on the part of the magician. But this rationalism is projected by the modern observer and does not belong to the primitive pattern. The existing evidence suggests that the magician, even when he is concerned with a utilitarian object like rain-making, is as remote from scientific positivism as the prophet to whom he is so closely related sociologically. The more primitive a culture is, the more difficult it is to distinguish the spell from the prayer or the magical technique from the religious ritual. Certainly there is good reason to believe that the Magdalenian cave paintings were magical in origin and were intended to promote success

[1] cf. Engels, *Ludwig Feuerbach* (tr. Martin Lawrence), pp. 30–1.

in the chase and to give the hunter power over the beasts. But we cannot assert that these rites were magical in an exclusive non-religious sense.

We know from modern evidence, above all from North America, that the magic of the hunter may be associated with strong religious beliefs and with intense religious feeling. Throughout the whole of North America, in spite of all differences of race and language, the culture of the hunters has been everywhere characterized by two dominant features—the importance of the vision or dream and the idea of the guardian spirit which is usually conceived in animal form.

The ultimate aims which the hunter hoped to secure were no doubt predominantly practical—success in hunting and success in war—but the means employed were of a definitely religious character—prayer and meditation, asceticism and withdrawal, humility and faith. " It was necessary," writes Miss R. Benedict, " to keep one's mind fixed upon the expected visitation. Concentration was the technique above all others upon which they relied. ' Keep thinking it all the time,' the old medicine men said always. Sometimes it was necessary to keep the face wet with tears so that the spirits would pity the sufferer and grant his request. ' I am a poor man. Pity me,' is a constant prayer. ' Have nothing,' the medicine men taught, ' and the spirits will come to you.' "[1]

Nothing could be further from Frazer's picture of the self-confident master of magical technique than this religious attitude which recalls the words of the Gospel: Blessed are the poor in spirit. Yet it is simpler and more primitive than the former which must be regarded either as an abstraction of modern theory, or as a specialized type which has developed out of the undifferentiated complex of magical and religious ideas. The religious magic of the primitive hunter is not a

[1] Ruth Benedict, *Patterns of Culture*, p. 82 (1935).

technique for the control of subhuman nature, but a means of communion with divine powers.

II

It was in this way—the way of initiation into divine mysteries —rather than by rational observation and logical thought that man first attained a conception of the order of nature.

Knowledge was the greatest and the most perilous gift of the gods, and nothing is more common in primitive myth and saga than the figure of the hero or the wise man who traverses the dangerous path between the two worlds and who by some heroic labour or sacrifice wrests from the gods the secret on which the welfare of mankind depends.

In our own Western culture, tradition, mystery and initiation are either so primitive that they are overlaid by more recent culture strata, as in the peasant survivals of vegetation magic and fertility rites; or they appear in a secondary form which is associated with a relatively advanced stage of religious development—as in the mystery religions of the Roman Empire.

In more primitive cultures, however, it is clear that mystery and initiation, whether we regard them as magical or religious, belong to the deepest and most universal level of thought and culture.

We find them in Australia and Melanesia in the form of puberty rites and totemic ceremonies; in North America and Siberia, in the training and discipline of the Shaman to acquire power by visionary experience; and in West Africa in the form of so-called fetishism and secret societies. Everywhere the knowledge which is regarded as indispensable for dealing with the vital affairs of life—for salvation in a pragmatic sense—is communicated by religious or magical rites accompanied by mythological and symbolic representations.

No doubt this knowledge may be objectively of little value; it may be false, superstitious and absurd. Nevertheless subjectively and psychologically it is the highest form of knowledge that primitive man possesses, and it is regarded as a tradition of sacred wisdom by which human life is governed. Therefore its cultural significance is of the highest importance, since it is the source and archetype of the tradition of higher knowledge out of which theology, philosophy and science developed in the course of the archaic culture.

In every culture and in every religion from the lowest to the highest we find three elements simultaneously present and organically related to one another.

In the first place there is the religious rite itself, which is usually but not necessarily a corporate social act; in the second place there is the myth which validates the ceremony by relating it to some religious belief and tradition; and finally there is the supernatural power or blessing which is the end of the sacred action and the fruit of the whole work.

In the institution of priesthood and sacrifice we see this threefold process worked out with complete logic and clarity, but it can be traced clearly enough in extremely primitive cultures, as in the totemic ceremonies of the natives of Australia or in the masked dances which play such an important part in the culture of primitive peoples all over the world.

There is, however, an important difference between the esoteric and the exoteric type of ceremony.

For example, in his study of the native cultures of California, Professor Kroeber distinguishes between those tribes like the Yuma and Mohave who have maintained a highly individualistic

and introverted cult of the dream vision as the source of supernatural power, and the more widespread cultures of central
California which practise initiation of the young men with
formal teaching and elaborate systems of religious ceremonial
and ritual dances. Finally in the north-west there is no secret
initiation and instruction, but the sacred dances are exoteric
ceremonies, which form the public accompaniment of the
esoteric act by which the priest performs a ceremony of world
renewal and " makes the world " for a new year.[1] Here in a
region of exceptionally backward and static culture we see
how there is already room for wide differences of religious
practice and organization, and to each of these corresponds a
specialized development of myth and doctrine (if one may use
the expression), culminating in northern California in the rites
of world renewal, and in the south in the organized cult of a
divine creator, who both ordered the world and instituted
the rites in which the initiates were instructed.

Every culture, in fact, develops its own religious techniques
for co-ordinating the life of society with the order of nature.
However low is his state of economic development, man is
always conscious of the cyclic character of the life of nature.
Even though he does not sow and reap the harvest, he is
conscious of winter and summer and day and night, of the
breeding times of the animals he hunts, and the ripening of the
plants and fruits which he collects. In the same way, however
rudimentary is his social organization, he is aware of birth and
death, and of the succession of generations. Therefore in his
religious life he attempts to co-ordinate the cycle of nature
with the cycle of human life. And the initiation ceremony
by which new members are aggregated or incorporated into
the community, and the seasonal ceremonies which are intended

[1] A. L. Kroeber, *Anthropology*, pp. 293-325 (1923).

to secure the food supply or to renew the life of nature, are the central points of the two cycles, which must somehow be brought together into an organic psychological unity.

We can see most clearly how this was done in our own tradition of Christian culture, where the feast of the Resurrection was associated on the one hand with the rite of the New Fire and on the other with the great annual ceremony of the Baptism of the neophytes. But a similar tendency to identify the cosmic and the social elements in the liturgical year can be traced back to the most primitive levels of culture. The initiation ceremony as a social act and the seasonal rites concerned with the food supply, with fertility or rain-making or the renewal of the year are distinct in nature and origin, but there is an almost universal tendency to bring them together, as we see in many forms of totemism and in the secret societies of West Africa, Melanesia and North America. Where this fusion is complete we get the developed type of the religious " mystery " with its several elements of initiation, instruction, sacred ritual and magical power or mystical communion.

The classical example of such a mystery is the myth of the Mother Goddess and the death and resurrection of her divine child or lover, the God of Vegetation, which is so familiar to us in its Sumerian, Anatolian and Syrian forms. And though these are the mature expression of a highly developed culture, they represent a pattern of myth and cult which goes back to the very beginnings of history and which has parallels and analogies at almost every known stage of culture. It has been argued by Sir William Ramsay, E. Hahn and others that the origins of agriculture and of the domestication of animals, especially the ox, arose out of this vegetation religion, so that in fact the art of agriculture was the fruit of the cult of the Mother Goddess and of the ritual imitation of the processes of nature, rather than the reverse.

Certainly there is reason to suppose that the veneration of the Mother Goddess as the principle of fertility goes back to palaeolithic times and thus far antedates the origins of agriculture; while on the other hand the clay figurines, etc., discovered by Garstang in 1935–6 at Jericho, suggest that in the neolithic culture of Palestine the development of agriculture and cattle breeding was associated with a fairly well-developed form of the religion of fertility and with a triad of three divine figures, one of which appears to represent the Mother Goddess.

III

But whatever the sequence of development may have been, it is clear that the rise of agriculture and cattle breeding as the economic basis of culture must have been accompanied both by a concentration of interest on the annual cycle of the life of nature and by an increased attention to the measurement of time, since the usual primitive reckoning by lunar months gives no sufficient guidance for the operations of the farmers' year. And with the observation of the solstices and the development of a solar calendar there went an increasing consciousness of the divine order of nature and of the dependence of the life of the earth on the order of the heavens. The science of the year and the calendar is perhaps the oldest and most venerable science that the human race has known. It is everywhere associated with the rise of the higher forms of civilization— alike in the Near East and the Far East and in Central America, with the Egyptians, the Sumerians, the Chinese and the Maya.

And everywhere it was regarded as a sacred science which was the peculiar province of the learned temple priesthoods.

The most remarkable example of this cult of the calendar is to be seen in the mysterious Maya culture which showed an extraordinary virtuosity in its solution of the problem of the calendar by an ingenious system of interlocking cycles based on the solar and planetary years. But it was the Sumerian and Egyptian developments which had the widest influence on world civilization, and it was these cultures that laid the foundations alike of the science of astronomy and the pseudo-science of astrology which were originally bound together so closely by their common religious basis. For the more men studied the stars the more they became impressed with the significance of the eternal order that ruled the movements of the heavenly bodies. And since they knew that the life of the earth and the succession of the seasons were governed by the sun and the moon, they concluded that the more remote and mysterious movements of the stars had a similar but more occult influence on the world and on human life and history. These powers were obviously divine. They were visible gods, and by contemplating them it was possible to discover the decrees of heaven and the fate of kingdoms and individuals.

This astral theology acquired immense prestige in antiquity and influenced not only the beginnings of science but also the classical tradition of philosophy. And it has a particularly close relation to the natural theology of Plato and Aristotle which is based on the principle that the nature of the stars is eternal and their movement derived from eternal and unmovable divinities. As Aristotle wrote, " our forefathers in the most remote ages have handed down to us their posterity a tradition, in the form of a myth, that these substances are gods and that the Divine encloses the whole of nature. The rest of the tradition has been added later in mythical form with a view to the persuasion of the multitude and to its legal and utilitarian expediency; they say these gods are in the form of men or like some of the other animals, and they say other things consequent on and similar to those which we have mentioned. But if we were to separate the first point from these additions

and take it alone—that they thought the first substances to be
gods, we must regard this as an inspired utterance and reflect
that, while probably each art and science has often been
developed as far as possible and has again perished, these
opinions have been preserved until the present, like relics of the
ancient treasure ".[1]

Thus in the Hellenic world the astral theology which had
been borrowed from Babylonia and enriched by the genius of
Greek philosophy ultimately produced the lofty but vague
ethical monotheism of Aratus[2] and Cleanthes and the later
Stoics. And the opening lines of Aratus' poem in particular
show how even at this advanced stage, where the natural
theology of the philosophers received its first endorsement
by a Christian apostle, the tradition still retains clear traces of
its source in the order of the calendar and the weeks and days
of the agricultural year.

Aratus writes:

" *From Zeus let us begin; him never do we men pass by*
In silence. Full of Zeus are all the streets,
And all the market-places of men; full is the sea,
And full the havens; sure at every turn we all have need of Zeus,
For we too are his offspring; and he, out of his kindness, gives to
   men
Auspicious omens, and doth wake the world to work,
Reminding men to earn their bread. He tells what time the clods
   are best
For ox and mattock; tells when the buxom season most invites

[1] *Metaphysics*. Book XII. Ch. VIII. Tr. W. D. Ross.
[2] Aratus was, like St. Paul, a native of Cilicia. He wrote his famous
poem at the Macedonian court, about 275 B.C. The popularity of his work
is shown by the commentary written by Hipparchus the astronomer, and
by the fact that such famous men as Cicero and Germanicus Caesar were
among its translators. His contemporary, Cleanthes, the author of a noble
hymn to Zeus, succeeded Zeno as the leader of the Stoic school in 263 B.C.

To plant the shoots and cast the seeds of every sort.
For himself it was who set the signs of heaven,
Marked out the constellations, and for the year contrived
What stars should best the heralds be
Of seasons to mankind, that so all things should grow unfailingly.
Wherefore men do reverence to him ever, first and last."[1]

Now as this genuine natural theology was not inconsistent with the fallacies and absurdities of the astrological theories with which it was intertwined, so too the barbarous mythologies of primitive polytheism were not inconsistent with a deep and true sense of the divine order of nature.

It is true that there is no obvious relation between the mythological and the scientific view of nature, and the myth has more in common with the dream image than with the logical concept. Primitive man saw the divine powers that rule the world in terrible or glorious shapes, like the masked dancers who figured in his ceremonial rites, and whatever forms he could imagine were but a pale reflection of the tremendous powers which manifested themselves in the strength of the bull and the light of the sun and the sound of the thunder.

The attempt to give symbolic or liturgical expression to the relation between these diverse divine powers gave rise to the theogonies and theogamies of the different mythological traditions, and it is precisely the rationalizing element in these divine pedigrees, as we see it for example in Hesiod, which brings out most strongly the non-rational character of the myth.

Nevertheless in spite of all the extravagance of mythological fantasy there was a tendency towards unity and order inherent in the religion of the archaic culture. The esoteric

[1] Aratus, *Phenomena*, 1-15. Tr. J. G. Frazer, *The Worship of Nature*, vol. I, 53 (1926).

traditions of the temple priesthoods tended to exalt the central object of their worship by making it the creator and source of all the other divine figures, or else treated the latter as different manifestations of the same deity. Thus the oldest written document of Egyptian religion, the so-called " Monument of Memphite Theology ", treats Ptah the divine craftsman of Memphis as the supreme creator, the heart and tongue of the gods who made all things and every divine word. " He fashioned the gods, he founded the Nomes, he set the gods on their holy places, he established their sacred revenues, he equipped their shrines, he made likenesses of their bodies as their hearts desired." " Everything has come forth from him whether food or nutrition or food of the gods or any good thing." Even the divine Ennead, the nine great gods of Memphis, are still in the mouth of Ptah, which pronounced the names of all things.[1]

And as an example of the other procedure we have the Babylonian Tablet of the Cossaean period (1500–1150 B.C.) which identifies all the greater Gods of Babylonia with the several functions of Marduk. Enlil is Marduk the King, Sin the Moon God is Marduk the Illuminator, Shamash the Sun God is Marduk the Judge and so forth.

In this way either by hierarchy or syncretism all the more developed forms of polytheism tend towards some kind of theological unity.

IV

Nevertheless this does not appear to have been the main source from which the idea of a cosmic order was developed. As we have seen in dealing with the institution of priesthood, the sacred science of sacrifice and ritual ceremony was the earliest organized form of human knowledge and the order of

[1] J. H. Breasted, *The Dawn of Conscience*, 29–42.

the religious ceremony was regarded in every society of archaic culture as the pattern and archetype of world order.

This is brought out, as I mentioned, with exceptional perfection and detail in the ritual theology of the Brahmanas. But it is far older than this, and the idea already finds expression in the hymns of the Rig Veda which are addressed to the great gods of the Aryans, to the divinized powers of nature and to the sacred fire and the sacred drink which are the centre of the earliest sacrificial ritual. The religion of the Rig Veda is perhaps the most perfect example of a polytheistic religion of the divine powers of nature that we know, and it is expressed with a poetic power and imagination which is unequalled except in Greek literature. Here as in the Homeric poems we seem to have a direct and untroubled vision of a heroic world peopled with divine figures conceived in the image of the warriors and princes who worshipped them. Nothing could seem further from the complicated ritualistic mysticism of the Brahmanas or from the introverted metaphysics of the Upanishads.

No doubt the gods are regarded as ruling over and intervening in human affairs, but they do not seem to belong to a different order of reality from that of nature. The Dawn which is addressed in some of the most beautiful of all ancient hymns is the real visible dawn rather than a supernatural power.

Nevertheless there is a power beyond the gods or at least beyond their anthropomorphic and naturalistic aspect, the divine order or *Rita* which governs alike the world of man and the world of the gods. This cosmic order is associated in particular with Varuna, the king of heaven, and with Agni the Lord of sacrifice. As the year is the Wheel of Rita with twelve spokes, so Agni, the sacred Fire, is its charioteer who " harnesses the steeds and holds the reins of Rita ".

Modern writers have been chiefly impressed by the moral

aspect of the concept, especially where it is related to Varuna as the righteous lord who is the protector of the laws of the gods.[1] But there can be no doubt that its real prototype is the ritual order, and that the order of the sacrifice, which one hymn speaks of as "the womb of the Rita",[2] was the basis on which the idea of a divine order pervading the universe and pre-serving the order of the seasons and the due relations of gods and men was developed.

Of course it is easy enough to explain away this development as the expression of the will to power of a highly organized class of priests or ritual technicians whose interest it was to exalt the prestige of the rites in which they possessed a mono-poly; and in India especially there is no doubt that this social factor did exercise a very important influence.

But it has much deeper roots than this. It represents a very simple and universal conviction which is basic to the archaic culture and is already present in some degree in much more primitive societies. It is the conviction that the powers that rule the earth and the powers that rule the year are governed or related by a common principle of order, and that man finds the key to this order, enters into active communion and participates in it in the ritual order of the sacrifice or the acted mystery. Unless we understand this principle, we cannot hope to understand the unity of ancient culture or to bridge the spiritual gulf which separates us from the pagan world.

For even the fundamental religious idea of divinity seems at first sight to have a completely different connotation in a polytheistic culture. In ancient Greece or India, as in modern Africa or Polynesia, one is struck by the apparently arbitrary and accidental way in which divinity is attributed to powers of the most diverse character. Almost anything can be a god,

[1] S.B.E. XLVI, 367, 370. Rig Veda I, XXIV, 9–10: XXV, 1–2.
[2] *ibid.*, 54, 220. Rig Veda I, LXV.

from the superhuman personalities who reign in heaven down to physical realities like rivers and mountains, from abstract powers like Wisdom and Speech down to material objects like the door and the hearth and the sacrificial ladle and the pressing stones. Thus the gods are both nearer to man and further from him than the God of the world religions.

They are beings of a higher order and superior power but by no means " wholly other " than man, as we see in Pindar's famous lines about the kinship of gods and men in the Nemaean Odes :

" One is the race of men, one is the race of gods, and from one mother do we both derive our breath; yet a power that is wholly sundered parteth us, in that the one is naught, while for the other the brazen heaven endureth as an abode un-shaken for evermore. Albeit, we mortals have some likeness, either in might of mind or at least in our nature, to the immortals, although we know not by what course, whether by day, no nor yet in the night watches, fate hath ordained that we should run."[1]

For men shared the same spiritual nature as the race of the gods, though only as it were by flashes, in the achievement of the hero or the inspiration of the prophet and the wise man. And gods and men alike were subject to a higher law, though the former were its guardians, the latter its servants. Behind the anthropomorphic divinities and the visible powers of nature there was the abstract conception of cosmic order or divine law—such as *Rita* in India, *Asha* in Persia, the Greek *Dike* and *Moira* and the Chinese *Tao*—out of which the gods emerged by mythology and ritual and into which they were re-absorbed by philosophy and theology.

[1] Nemaean Odes, VI, 1.

V

The pre-Socratic tradition of Greek philosophy is above all an attempt to explain the nature of the unity of the cosmic process of which men were already conscious religiously. In the early Ionian and Italian philosophy—notably with the Pythagoreans and Heracleitus and Empedocles—we see the religious conception of a sacred order reinterpreted as an esoteric teaching concerning the true nature of the cosmic process. " Wisdom," says Heracleitus, " is one thing. It is to know the thought (or word) by which all are steered through all." " This order which is the same for all things, no one of the gods or men has made; but it was ever, is now, and ever shall be, an ever-living Fire, by measures kindling and by measures going out." " Even the sun will not exceed his measures; if he does, the Erinyes, the avenging handmaids of Justice, will find him out."

" Men have made a law for themselves, not knowing what they made it about, but the gods have ordered all things. Now the arrangements that men have made are never constant, neither when they are right, nor when they are wrong. But the arrangements which the gods have made are always right both when they are right and when they are wrong; so great is the difference."

" Wisdom is common to all things. Those who speak with intelligence must hold fast to the common, as a city holds fast to its laws and even more strongly. For all human laws are fed by one law, the Divine; it prevails as much as it will and suffices for all things and something to spare."[1]

These quotations show that in spite of his contempt for " the mystery mongers and magians, priests of Bacchus and

[1] Tr. J. Burnet, *Early Greek Philosophy* (1892), pp. 133–42, Nos. 19, 20, 29, 61, 91.

priestesses of the wine vat ", Heracleitus was himself a religious thinker—a theologian in the Greek sense of the word—who revealed the mystery of the divine word in cryptic oracular utterances which are prophetic rather than rationalistic in character. And this religious element is even more evident in Empedocles who habitually clothes his thought in mythological figures. With Empedocles also we have the clearest possible assertion of the prophetic character and divine vocation of the philosopher. He himself claims divine honours and asks if it is any great matter that he should surpass mortal and perishable men. For he is one of the purified and enlightened souls who " at the last appear among mortal men as prophets, poets, healers, and princes; and thence they rise up as gods exalted in honour sharing the hearth of the other gods and the same table, free from human woes, safe from destiny and incapable of hurt ".[1]

In all this there is much that reminds us of the development of Indian thought when the polytheism of the Rig Veda was becoming transformed into the religious metaphysics of the Upanishads. But in early Greek philosophy the attention of the thinker is still concentrated on the order of nature rather than on the nature of the soul. Pre-Socratic philosophy is in fact essentially a Natural Theology, in the sense of a doctrine of the divine order of nature.

It is a *via media* between the irrational mythology of the traditional religion and the irreligious rationalism which was already beginning to attract the Western mind.

No doubt philosophy itself became one of the most important influences in the secularization of Greek culture, just as the Natural Theology of the seventeenth and eighteenth centuries was used as an agent of secularization by the rationalism of the French Enlightenment. But this is no justification for ignoring

[1] Tr. Burnet, *op. cit.* p. 237.

the existence of a profoundly religious element in the thought of Heracleitus, Empedocles, Xenophanes and the Pythagoreans, any more than the rationalism of the Encyclopaedist should cause us to under-estimate the religious element in the thought of Leibnitz or Malebranche or the Cambridge Platonists.

The conception of a sacred science of the order of nature which has its roots so deep in the underworld of primitive magic, did not vanish with the birth of Greek science in the sixth century B.C. It continued to flourish in the classical age and bore fruit not only in the scientific mysticism of the Pythagoreans, but in the philosophy of Plato and later in the teachings of the Stoics, through whom it passed into the common tradition of Graeco-Roman culture. In its later phases it acquired an even closer relation to metaphysics and to Natural Theology as a result of the encyclopaedic scholasticism of the Neoplatonic school of Alexandria, which created an elaborate synthesis of Greek science and philosophy under the later Roman Empire and during the early Byzantine period.

It was in this form that the Greek scientific tradition was handed on to the mediaeval world both in the East and the West. It was not regarded as the fragmentary remains of a vanished culture, but as a single universal body of knowledge which had been handed down as an intact deposit of ancient wisdom. We have only to read the *Divina Commedia* or the *Convivio* of Dante to see how this tradition fused physics, metaphysics and theology into an organic unity in which the order of the world reflects the hierarchy of spiritual being. And remote as this cosmological mysticism may appear from the modern scientific tradition, it was not without its influence on the minds of men like Copernicus and Kepler and the other leaders of the scientific Renaissance in the sixteenth and seventeenth centuries.

Indeed the Natural Theology of Humanism preserved the spirit of the Hellenistic-Mediaeval synthesis throughout the formative centuries in which the foundations of modern science were laid, and it provided the spiritual background of the new physics and cosmology. In spite of the revolutionary transformation of these sciences in that age, the Western mind was still dominated by the Hellenic ideal of the world as a true cosmos which is intelligible to scientific reason because it is the work of Divine Reason which reaches from end to end mightily and orders all things well.

The Divine Order and the Social Order. Sacred Law

THE IMPORTANCE of Law in the history of culture. Law antecedent to the State. Sacred character of Law in all known cultures. Survival of this conception in modern times as a direct legacy of the classical and humanist tradition of Natural Theology. Twofold source of primitive law: law as hallowed custom and law as divine decree. Divination and law. Law and Tabu. The complete fusion of social order and sacred order in the theocratic type of archaic culture, such as survives in a fossilized form in the Pueblo culture of the south-west of North America. Contrast of this type with the aggressive dynamic warrior culture which stresses personal leadership and prestige more than conformity to the sacred order. Interaction of these two types in the history of culture. Fusion of the two types in a single society, the unity of which is preserved by the institution of sacred kingship. China as the classical example of a world civilization which has maintained the ideal of a sacred order in its strict archaic sense. Confucianism and the Sacred Rites. Co-ordination of the moral order and the cosmic order. The tradition of theocratic monarchy and Confucian rationalism. Permanence and importance of the influence of the Confucian scholars in Chinese civilization comparable to that of the Brahmins in Indian culture.

CHAPTER VIII

The Divine Order and the Social Order.
Sacred Law

I

THE SACRED order which man has seen in the order of nature and in the order of the sacrifice is also seen as the law or norm which rules human society. This concept has exerted an extraordinarily deep influence on culture, which has endured even to the present day, and it is here, perhaps, that it is easiest to trace the continuity between the sacred order of primitive and archaic thought and modern philosophic Natural Theology.

For the revolutionary changes which heralded the coming of the modern state were consciously and avowedly based on the idea of the priority of the Natural Law, and when Dupont de Nemours speaks of the Declaration of the Rights of Man as " the fundamental law of the laws of our own and of other nations which ought to last as long as time itself ", he was speaking the same language that had been used for thousands of years by theologians and Fathers of the Church, by Roman jurists and Greek philosophers. All of them speak of the Law of Nature as the eternal norm to which all human laws must conform and from which they derive their ultimate moral sanction. And though the nineteenth century saw a strong positivist reaction against natural law both from the utilitarian and the historical schools, this reaction has not proved entirely successful even from the lawyer's point of view, and during the present generation there has been a definite revival and rehabilitation of the tradition of the law of nature.

Now behind the philosophic idea of natural law, there is the much older theological idea that law is not a purely political or social creation, but requires a divine sanction and origin in order to make it truly law. It is therefore not the State but God who is the source of all law, and the kings and the judges are not so much law makers as vindicators and guardians of the unchanging decrees of justice to which they are themselves subject. As Professor Kern has shown in his studies on Kingship and Law in the Middle Ages,[1] legal reform and the promulgation of new laws were always regarded in theory as a return to an already existent standard—a restoration of the " good old laws " of King Edward the Confessor or some similar canonized figure of ideal kingship. It was like a restoration of the true standard of the coinage after it had become temporarily debased.

No doubt mediaeval Christendom, like Islam, was influenced by Jewish tradition which insisted on the historic fact of a divine law that had been formally promulgated by an act of divine revelation. But the concept of divine legislation is by no means peculiar to Judaism. It is to be found in one form or another in all the world religions and in all the ancient civilizations. Even when, as in classical Greece, the figure of a human legislator like Lycurgus or Solon becomes more prominent, it does not by any means result in a secularization of the idea of law. The laws are " the discovery and gift of the gods " and the human legislator is the spokesman or teacher by whom the order of justice was revealed and made plain. The secularization of law in Greece was like the secularization of philosophy. If they were rationalized, reason itself was divinized,

[1] F. Kern, *Kingship and Law in the Middle Ages*, trans. and ed. S. B. Chrimes (Oxford, 1939).

and the lawgiver and the philosopher never entirely lost their sacred and prophetic character.

Thus throughout the history of Western culture from classical antiquity through the Christian Middle Ages down to modern liberal and humanist civilization, we find a consistent development of the concept of law as something which transcends political expediency and human will and is grounded on external reality; or as the classical eighteenth century formulation has it, " on the Eternal Reason and Proportion of things " that is " the order by which the Universe subsists."[1]

But this conception is not peculiar to a single historic tradition of thought and culture. It is to be found in all cultures and in all systems of thought. Everywhere what is socially lawful and unlawful is related to what is morally right and wrong, and everywhere the moral law is based ultimately on religious sanctions. If we leave the historic cultures and go back to the most elementary and primitive types of society known to us, we find the relation between religion and the social order even closer and more immediate than it is in an advanced civilization. The rules by which the life of a primitive community is governed—the rules of kinship and marriage, the constitution of authority and the principles of social organization, crime and penalty and the general rules for the wellbeing of society—are all sacred rules enforced by religious sanctions. These rules belong normally to two different types. On the one hand, there is the rule of custom, guarded and handed down by the elders or the priests, which is often regarded as a sacred tradition originating from the divine ancestors of the community. And on the other hand, there is the exceptional decision or judgment which is obtained directly from the gods by divination or by the consultation of an oracle.

[1] By Samuel Clarke in his refutation of Hobbes in the Boyle Lectures for 1705 *On Natural Religion*.

For in one form or another the practice of divination is universal among all primitive peoples, as well as throughout the archaic cultures and in the higher civilizations down to the coming of the world religions.

In his massive study of witchcraft and divination among the Azande on the border of the Congo and the Anglo-Egyptian Sudan Dr. Evans Pritchard has shown in the case of a modern people how every detail of life is governed and directed by the decision of the poison oracle.[1] The Azande are not a particularly religious people—rather the reverse—and their system of divination is not integrated in a theological or mythological system. But if we turn to the other side of Africa—to a people to whom I have already referred more than once—we find that the oracle has become a great god—Ifa—and his cult is the sacred centre of the whole Yoruba culture.

In either case nothing could be further from the developed conception of natural law than the practice of divination; where the one appeals to the social super-ego, the latter is a technique of direct appeal to unknown and supernatural forces. And in the same way the sanctions and penalties which are involved by the breach of sacred custom or the infringement of a sacred precept are equally irrational in character.

The man who forsakes the safe way of ancestral custom, who disregards the verdict of the gods or who infringes the sacred order is exposed to terrible spiritual dangers. He is the " impious " man, the archetype of the sinner and the criminal who is at once the object of divine vengeance and human abhorrence. It is difficult to exaggerate the tremendous force of this primitive sense of guilt and supernatural penalty which is so prominent in ancient mythology and ritual and which has entered so largely into the modern psychological terminology

[1] E. E. Evans Pritchard, *Witchcraft, Oracles and Magic among the Azande* (Oxford, 1937).

of the unconscious. But it is not difficult for us to comprehend it, since it still survives in the literary traditions of tragedy and in the basic religious concept of sin. And in an entirely different context we see in the institution of Tabu how a sacred prohibition enforced by supernatural sanctions may be incorporated into the social pattern as an instrument of kingly power and majesty without losing its non-rational character and appeal. The divinity which hedged kings or nobles could be communicated to their surroundings and belongings and manipulated at their will so that it became a regular technique of social control. And this made such an impression on the early European travellers that the word taboo has been adopted into English and other European languages in an extended sense to describe any irrational prohibition enforced by supernatural sanctions. But even in its authentic sense Tabu has a sufficiently close affinity with the Latin *sacer* and *consecratio*—words which held so important a place in early Roman religion and law. Everywhere in fact the sacred and the prohibited are organically connected as positive and negative aspects of the same power. The man who infringes a sacred restriction or interferes with a sacred rite lets loose forces of destruction which may be fatal to himself and even to the community.

Hence the fact that many primitive societies seem to be deficient in political organization and almost devoid of definite legal institutions does not mean that they are lawless or that they lack organs of social control. On the contrary, primitive society is hedged in by a complicated system of prohibitions and restrictions and finds its security in a strict adherence to the law of custom and the guidance of divination. In other words the element of social control is provided by religion and ritual and magic rather than by political and legal organization.

157

II

And as civilization advances, though there is certainly a development of political authority and legal institutions, the greatest advances seem to have been achieved by those societies which specialized in the study and cultivation of a sacred order, *i.e.* the societies of the archaic culture. From the nature of the case we have no adequate evidence of the religious life of these societies before the invention of writing, which was one of their culminating achievements, but we can find comparable social types in existing societies which are furthest removed in space from the great centres of diffusion of the archaic culture in the Old World. Thus in the case of the Pueblo culture of New Mexico we have a most remarkable example of a society based on the sacred ritual order, which has endured almost intact, while the surrounding native peoples and cultures that were far more fluid and apparently capable of adaptation to new conditions have withered and practically disappeared. This is an almost perfect example of a society or group of societies governed by an elaborate ceremonial order administered by a number of priesthoods or religious corporations whose ceremonial observances occupy the major part of the time and the attention of the community.

It is impossible to find a more completely socialized type of culture, in which every activity and every emotion have their appointed place which does not change from year to year or from generation to generation. But this exact and meticulous social conformity is obtained without the intervention of political authority or coercive law. The element of organized power, the strictly political element in society is reduced to a minimum. The Pueblo community is a pure theocracy in which the authority of the priests is based directly on the sacred order of which they are the ministers. Even economic interests

158

are subordinated to religious considerations, and a man's prestige and social importance depend not on his wealth but on knowledge of ritual and his inherited prerogatives in the ceremonial order.

This type of society strikes the modern Western observer merely as an interesting curiosity to be studied in the same way as he studies any archaic survival. But its real importance consists in the fact that it preserves in almost unadulterated purity an element which exists in every culture but which can seldom be seen and studied in isolation. Everywhere the development of civilization has been based on the conception of a sacred order and has used theocratic forms of social organization, but in most civilizations this element has co-existed with the more " secular " principles of economic wealth and political power from which so much of the driving force of social change has been derived.

Aggression, war, striving for power, self assertion and competition—all contradict or clash with the theocratic ideal of submission to the sacred law and strict individual conformity to the ritual order. Yet they are the dynamic forces which tend to shape the actual social world. Here again the example of the Pueblo culture is particularly illuminating because it exists in immediate local contact and spiritual contrast with the culture of the Apaches and the Indians of the Plains, which is as warlike and aggressive as any culture known to us.

These cultures are certainly not irreligious, but their religion stresses precisely the opposite qualities to those of the Pueblo culture. It stresses the personal experience of the individual, as represented by the dream vision, which is the pledge and reward of personal prowess in war or in hunting. The tribe lived for war, and the position of the war leader and the individual champion or guerilla fighter was the centre of social prestige, power and wealth.

The culture of the Pueblos, however, was not only more

advanced, it was also more enduring than that of the Indians of the Plains. It shows that it is possible for a society to maintain itself through the ages without internal decadence on a strictly theocratic basis without appealing to the dynamism of aggression and competition. On the other hand, it remained static, without any considerable tendency to expand—indeed rather the reverse; while the Indians of the Plains expanded very rapidly over an immense extent of territory, and for a time pressed hard on the higher civilization of the Pueblo peoples. And further south in Mexico the highest native civilization of the Continent was attained when a warrior people from the north overran a higher civilization of the theocratic type which had been developed by the Maya, and thus produced the complex blend of theocratic and warrior elements which characterized the Aztec culture. But the result of this blending of two opposite types of culture was an extreme development of ritual human sacrifice which made the Aztec cult perhaps the most sanguinary and inhuman form of worship that has ever existed.

Thus in the New World we see the characteristic types of religious culture more sharply defined, and developed in more exaggerated forms than in the Old. Everywhere, however, we can trace a similar pattern of development: (1) a relatively pacific and highly socialized theocratic culture based on the ritual order; (2) an aggressive warrior culture which stimulated individual prowess and personal honour in both the social and the religious order and (3) finally a crossing or synthesis of the two in which the theocratic element is represented by the priesthood and the warlike element by the nobles, while the institution of divine or sacred kingship provides a bond of union between the two social traditions.

It is this synthesis of the priestly and warrior societies which has been the dominant form of culture throughout the Old

World during historic times. And it still exists to-day, in so far as modern society has not been completely secularized. And in the historic European and Asiatic forms of the state it is still possible to trace the conflict and compromise between the theocratic conception of law as conformity to a sacred super-human order and the " political " conception of the state as a secular organization of material power and coercive authority.

III

(i)

But while all the higher cultures are of the third type, and represent a synthesis of theocratic and warrior traditions, they differ widely in the relative importance of the two elements and in the complexity of their structure. And among the great world civilizations that have survived to modern times, none possesses such a degree of continuity and autarky as the civilization of China. Through all the changes and revolutions of their history, the Chinese people have remained masters of their destiny and have shown a power of absorbing alien elements and resisting foreign influences such as no other people has ever possessed. And this resistant and enduring character of Chinese culture has been due in no small degree to the fidelity with which it has preserved the sacred order and followed the ancestral rites.

Now at first sight it might seem that China is the very opposite of what is usually meant by a theocratic society. There are few historic civilizations in which the priesthood has played a smaller part than in China: indeed it is usually re-garded as the least religious and the most secular of all the great world cultures (leaving out of account the development of Western culture in very recent times). But though China has never been a theocratic civilization in the sense of a civilization that is governed by a priesthood, it has been more than any other a culture based on the Natural Law.

In China alone do we find an unbroken continuity between the primitive conception of a sacred order, which manifests itself alike in the order of nature, the order of the sacrifice and the social order, and the fully developed philosophic conception of a moral law by which the life of the individual is co-ordinated with the life of society, and both alike are subordinated to the law that rules the universe. Nor has this been an abstract intellectual development: it was the living tradition of the whole society, which has been embodied in the institutions and laws, the state and the family, and has inspired some of the greatest achievements of Chinese culture.

Thanks to this continuity of tradition, we find in China, and in China alone, all the characteristic features of the religion of the archaic culture preserved at least formally intact in one of the most highly developed and refined forms of civilization the world has known. Down to 1912 the Emperor still offered the great sacrifice of the winter solstice at the Altar of Heaven with all the ritual of a remote, almost prehistoric past, and every spring he performed the ceremony of the sacred ploughing which opened the agricultural year. For the ancient Chinese religion like that of the other archaic societies was based on the principle of a perfect co-ordination of the heavenly and the earthly orders by a cycle of ritual actions: (1) the ordering of the year and the seasons; (2) the ensuring of the fertility of the earth and (3) the propitiation of the divine ancestors; above all (4) the obtaining of guidance from above in order to steer the state securely along the path of the sacred order: all these ends were obtained, as in the Pueblo culture, by the exact performance of the annual cycle of the sacred rites.

But it is extremely unlikely that a religion thus identified with the order of nature and the worship of nature would have survived the competition of world religions like Buddhism and the criticism of the philosophers and the sceptics, if it had not been for the work of the great moral teacher and reformer who has made such a deep and enduring impression on Chinese thought and culture.

Confucius was no prophet; he claimed no new revelation. He was a traditionalist *par excellence*, one who prided himself on being " a transmitter and not an originator, a believer in and lover of antiquity ". Yet he has always been reckoned as one of the founders of the world religions, like Buddha or Zarathustra; and not without reason, since he transformed the archaic nature religion of ancient China into a religious philosophy and a moral law that have ruled the mind of China ever since.

The spirit of the Confucian teaching is dominated by the conception of a sacred order which governs the life of society as well as the life of nature. This order has been handed down from the holy founders of Chinese civilization by ancestral tradition, it was embodied in the sacred rites of which Confucius was a devoted student, and it found further corroboration and definition in the science of divination, the principles of which are contained in the *Book of Changes*.

All political power and authority was derived from this divine order by the Mandate of Heaven which was given and withdrawn by the sovereign decrees of providence according to the virtue or the fault of the ruler and his officers; but any breach of order at any point in the social hierarchy from the top to the bottom was liable to disturb the sacred harmony and provoke the anger of Heaven.

All this was part of the religious inheritance of the archaic Chinese culture which Confucius accepted in a spirit of filial reverence, and it is difficult for us to make distinctions between

163

the Confucian doctrine and the archaic tradition, since all our knowledge of the latter is derived from the teaching of the Confucian school itself.

In the age of Confucius this archaic tradition was already in process of decay. The theocratic order of the old feudal empire was dissolving into a chaos of warring states which were increasingly dominated by sheer power politics. But the work of Confucius was not confined to the idealization of a vanished past, it involved the transformation of the old conception of the sacred ritual order into a new principle of ethical order which became the heart of Chinese civilization. For Confucius taught that it was not enough to maintain the external order of ritual and law, unless man conformed himself to it with the complete adhesion of his mind and will. Without the virtues of disinterested goodness and sincerity and loyalty, the venerable cycle of the sacred rites is deprived of its spiritual efficacy. Thus the Confucian education was an intensive process of moral discipline which aimed at creating not merely scholars in the European sense of the word, but " superior men " *i.e.*, members of a spiritual élite.

The Chinese system of spiritual values is so different from our own that it is very hard to find an adequate equivalent for any of the classical Chinese moral concepts in Western speech which does not deprive them of their religious associations or their spiritual atmosphere, and it is only too easy to translate what the Confucians regarded as a profound expression of spiritual wisdom into an arid moral platitude. In the first age of Confucianism, however, there is no doubt that the attitude of the teacher towards moral training and social duty and knowledge of the Rites was more comparable to the attitude of a monk towards the Holy Rule and the Divine Liturgy than it is to the attitude of a Western scholar towards humane letters and philosophy.

For behind the meticulous traditionalism and the cere-monial morality of the early Confucian tradition there is a genuine piety and a religious adoration of the sacred order, manifested in the Decrees of Heaven, the Sacred Rites and the law of duty.

It is true that there is a strange lack in the Confucian teaching of theological doctrine and theistic devotion. But this is not a sign of religious scepticism or of a rationalist attitude, it is a part of the extreme reserve and distrust of unregulated private feelings which characterize Confucian thought.

All man's relations to the powers above are determined by the Sacred Rites. The Rites have their origin in Heaven. By them the divine rulers of old executed the purposes of Heaven towards man and rectified man's natural tendencies. Those who disregard the Rites, perish: those who observe them, prosper. Anyone who tries to go beyond the Rites by entering into personal relations with divine powers or seeking knowledge which Heaven has not revealed is guilty of impiety and incurs the anger of Heaven, just as the subject who disre-gards the etiquette of the court and meddles in the affairs of the state outside his proper office is worthy of condemnation and punishment.

Hence the emphasis of Confucian religion is not on the supernatural and the esoteric, but on the Rites, and on be-haviour and the fulfilment of social duty. That every man should do his duty in that state of life to which it has pleased Heaven to call him is the essence of Confucianism. It may seem to us a slight foundation on which to build a world religion, but as a system of social ethics and a rule of culture the founda-tions laid by Confucius and the Confucian scholars have out-lasted the rise and fall of civilizations and religions.

The reason of this enduring quality is not merely the

165

traditionalism of Chinese civilization which is its effect rather than its cause. It is due rather to the strength of the psychological motives to which Confucianism appeals and to the way in which it relates its doctrine of universal order and its theory of the state to the primary elements of social relationship represented by the patriarchal family. The canonization of filial piety as the great Confucian virtue provided a perfect psychological basis for the paternal authority of the Confucian state and the ceremonial piety of the state religion.

As the emperor, the Son of Heaven, performs the great annual sacrifices in a spirit of filial piety and affection, so the people approaches the emperor, and the head of a family the representative of authority, and the individual the head of his clan and family. All social relationships are bound together by this single all-embracing attitude of filial piety which makes the family a microcosm reflecting the order of the empire and the order of Heaven.

If these three could be co-ordinated by the virtue of the ruler and the virtue of the subject and the practice of the Rites, then the sacred order of the Divine Sages (" the founding fathers " if one may borrow an American expression), would return and " the Great Unity " or cosmic harmony be attained.

Thus the Confucian ideal of society is definitely theocratic: a government by the spiritual power by means of the ritual order. " If you govern the people by regulations and keep order by punishment, they will flee from you and lose their sense of shame," says the Master, " but if you govern them by spiritual power (*Te*) and keep order by the Rites, they will be shame-faced and come to you of their own accord." And again " He who governs by his spiritual power is like the Pole Star which abides in its place while all the stars bow towards it ".[1]

[1] The Analects of Confucius, II, i and iii.

(ii)

Confucius never attempted to deny the transcendent character of the sacred order. He sought only to make it a living principle of social behaviour and personal conduct instead of the esoteric lore of diviners and priests.

Nevertheless this esoteric doctrine of the sacred order, which finds its classical expression in the writings of the Taoist philosophers, was hardly less important for the history of Chinese thought than the Confucian tradition itself. And though it developed to diametrically opposite conclusions, it had its origins in the same basic conceptions of the archaic culture which inspired the ritual traditionalism of Confucius.

The Taoists believed no less than the Confucians in the existence of a universal order to which man must conform himself in order to fulfil his destiny. Like the Confucians, they regarded this order as manifested in the course of nature, above all in the stars, and in music; and both agreed in their use of divination by means of the tortoise shell, and the sacred diagrams of the *Book of Changes*, through which they believed that the Way of Heaven was made known to men.

They differed only in the application of this fundamental idea, for while the Confucians strove to conform themselves to the cosmic order by an active moral discipline and the observance of ceremonial rites, the Taoists sought the same end by mystical contemplation and the practice of magic and alchemy.

It seems probable that the traditional account of the origin of the two schools has a considerable element of truth. According to this view, the Ju, the scholars, were the successors of the officials of the Imperial Chancery of the Chou Dynasty who superintended the public economy and social order of the state, whereas the predecessors of the Taoists were the astrologers and divines who were attached to the Third

167

Ministry, which superintended public worship and divination.

Thus the two traditions would represent two specialized techniques each with its own corresponding ritual practices and moral ideals. The Rites of the Confucians were public and social, their morals were a social ethic, their ideal was the perfect citizen, "the superior man" or "gentleman" of Confucius. On the other hand the Taoists placed their ideal of conduct not in the observance of rites and ceremonies and in a painstaking obedience to moral precepts but in a mystical quietism by which man conformed himself to the divine order of nature. Hence their criticism of the artificial character of Confucian ethics, their hostility to the niceties of ceremonial etiquette and their ridicule of the Confucian cult of the precedents of antiquity.

They compared the efforts of the disciples of Confucius to restore the ancient usages to an attempt to dress up a monkey in the robes of one of the princes of antiquity. The monkey remains a monkey, and the fine robes only accentuate its absurdity. Above all they condemned the futile optimism of the pedants who attempted to restore the golden age by external means.

Chuang Tzu, one of the greatest of the early Taoists, writes—" The wise men have squared up the empire with the axe and the saw. They have applied the hammer and the chisel to men's morals." And what is the result? " To-day we see the corpses of the condemned piled up in heaps, those who carry the cangue pass in long files, everywhere one sees men condemned to different punishments. And amidst all these atrocities, among the handcuffs, the shackles and the implements of torture, the disciples of Confucius and Mo Tzu stand on their toes to look important, and turn up their sleeves complacently in admiration for their work. How extreme is the obduracy of these men, how boundless is their impudence!

Does the cangue sum up the wisdom of the sages? Are the handcuffs, shackles and tortures the expression of their benevolence and equity? Are not these statesmen more maleficent than the most infamous tyrants in history? There is truth in the proverb which says 'Exterminate wisdom, destroy science, and the empire will return to order of its own accord.' " [1]

This passage gives some idea of the revolutionary spirit of the great Taoist writers of the third century B.C. Chuang Tzu and Lieh Tzu were not simply religious mystics, they were metaphysical nihilists and political anarchists. They taught that civilization is corruption, that law creates criminals, wealth makes thieves and philosophy bad men. " It is the love of knowledge," says Chuang Tzu, " which has caused this disorder in men's nature. It has lasted since the Three Dynasties (of antiquity). For eighteen hundred years men have been accustomed to turn up their noses at natural simplicity and to think highly of ritual quackery. They have got accustomed to preferring verbose and deceitful politics to frank and loyal inactivity. It is the talkers who have brought ruin on the world."

But while the propaganda of the Taoists destroyed the prestige of Confucian idealism, it was not the mystics who were the gainers. Their anti-traditional ideas were taken up and used for very different ends by the new school of Legal Positivists—the Fa Hia—which inspired the brilliant and ruthless statesmen who created the Empire of Ts'in in the third century B.C. They taught that Virtue is Power and that states acquire Power not by correct ritual and traditional morality but by the political instruments of war and law. The people is clay and the maker of the laws is the potter and the vessel is hardened in the kiln of war.

[1] Chuang Tzu. Ch. XI., tr. L. Wieger, S.J. *Les Pères du Système Taoiste*, 285-7 (Hien Hien, 1913).

Every man seeks his own ease and profit. Therefore the statesman must institute a system of rewards and inexorable punishments which will make it impossible for any man to find any ease or profit except in the service of the state. Make the law of the state after the pattern of the Law of Heaven: uniform, irresistible, inexorable, without pity for the weak and without indulgence for the strong. For law is the true Tao, the mother of states.

In spite of a superficial veneer of Taoist ideas, this doctrine of the Chinese positivists was as completely irreligious as that of any school of thought in any age or country. It shows the result of the attempt to separate the principle of social order from personal morality and from all theological sanctions and base it exclusively on external utilitarian standards. And it is significant that this drastic secularization of Chinese culture and the abandonment of the sacred order was accompanied by a ruthless form of militarism, entirely alien from the classical Chinese tradition. The application of the principles of the legal positivists to practical politics produced a predatory imperialism which deluged China in blood.

In spite of the unwilling admiration which later generations of scholars felt for the statesmen and warriors who created the Chinese empire, they felt at the same time that Ts'in was a cannibal state which paid its soldiers scalp-money for every head cut off and lived by devouring its neighbours.

The great and sinister figure who was the First Emperor, Shih Huang Ti, has always been regarded by the scholars as an example of the successful tyrant, a man whose boundless pride and disregard for moderation, tradition and reverence was a challenge to Heaven. The creator of the Empire and the builder of the Great Wall was also the Burner of the Books and the persecutor of the Confucian scholars; and the destruction of his work a few years after his death was mainly due to the fact that it was not rooted in the sacred order of tradition but in the triumphant will of an overweening genius.

When order was restored under the Han, the Confucian scholars once more took up their work of moral education after the traditional pattern of the classics and the sacred Rites.

Again and again throughout Chinese history after a temporary phase of militarism or the temporary triumph of Taoism or Buddhism, we find the scholars bringing China back once more to the perennial teaching of the Confucian ethics and the sacred order of the past.

And the result has been that in China alone among the advanced civilizations of the world the law of nature has not been a philosophical abstraction but a living force which has had a religious appeal to the heart and conscience of the people.

It is true that Confucianism is not a religion in the full sense of the word, but it represents an essential part of religion which has nowhere else been cultivated so persistently or with such social profit.

In this way Chinese civilization seems to have solved certain fundamental problems of the social and moral order more successfully than any other known culture. No doubt this achievement is counterbalanced by corresponding failures and defects, both in the religious tradition and in the social order. For example, the excessive emphasis on the patriarchal pattern of authority and tradition has always exposed China to the danger of a destructive social crisis whenever there is a change of dynasty or a loss of prestige and efficiency on the part of the government.

And even more serious is the lack of satisfaction for the religious needs of the individual which leaves a spiritual void at the heart of Chinese culture. This explains the part which Buddhism has played in China as a secondary unofficial religion which has co-existed with the official Confucian cult.

But in so far as this substitute has been effective, it has tended to destroy the spiritual unity of the culture, since from the Confucian standpoint Buddhism is no more than an anti-social superstition.

Yet in spite of all that can be said on the other side, it is difficult to over-estimate the achievement of the Confucian tradition. It has ensured the unbroken continuity of Chinese culture for thousands of years so that nothing in the past is alien from the present, and the whole world of thought and society from its legendary beginnings to its existing form is dominated by the same moral values, the same laws of thought and the same code of manners and behaviour.

To the Western mind this spectacle of a civilization and a whole world governed by the old school tie—even though it be that of the school of Lu[1]—may appear a somewhat alarming spectacle. Nevertheless Confucian scholars or literati who have been the schoolmasters of China succeeded in preserving the vitality of Chinese civilization through the ages, while younger and more aggressive cultures have withered and disappeared.

The order of Confucian scholars has been the most successful example in history of a spiritual organ which is perfectly adapted to its social function. No doubt the Brahmin tradition in India is even older and no less enduring, but the Brahmins have been a privileged sacred caste without any direct responsibility for the social welfare of their community. In the Confucian tradition, social privilege has never been divorced from social responsibility, and the spiritual power, as represented by the scholars, has been the principle of unity, continuity and moral leadership in Chinese society.

[1] Lu was the little feudal state in Shan Tung to which Confucius belonged and where he established his school after his return from exile.

The Divine Order and the Spiritual Life.
The Way of Perfection

SPIRITUAL culture—the discipline of the soul or the interior life—an integral part of true culture. Importance attached to asceticism and spiritual training in primitive cultures. The training of the Shaman. Asceticism and training in ancient India. The quest for salvation and the development of disciplines of salvation. Karma and the chain of existence. Deliverance from the body the aim of life. Deliverance by intellectual intuition. Deliverance by moral discipline. The Buddhist discipline of salvation as a theory of negation and as a positive social force. Asoka. Theistic tendencies of later Buddhism. Tendency of all the great ancient and mediaeval cultures to regard the way of salvation and a spiritual intuition as the ultimate goal of all human culture. Unresolved dualism between the world negation of the contemplative and the moral and social discipline of the order of culture.

The Divine Order and the Spiritual Life. The Way of Perfection

I

(i)

HUMAN culture involves a discipline of the mind and the spirit as well as a social discipline. This is so obvious that it is evident in the very history of the word. For in our own civilization the primary meaning of the word culture has always been the cultivation of the mind through the higher forms of education so that "the man of culture" was one who possessed a general familiarity with the classical tradition of literature and scholarship. In this restricted sense of the word, culture would seem to have little to do with religion. Indeed in the West, culture and religion have often been regarded as independent spheres which might be mutually hostile or exclusive. Ever since the time of Tertullian and the early Christians there has been a type of intellectual puritanism which is distrustful of literary culture and insists on the opposition between the wisdom of the saints and all secular science and culture. This however is a development that is peculiar to Western civilization and has its roots in the historical dualism between Christianity and Hellenism and between the Bible and classical literature—a dualism which was accentuated by the Humanism of the Renaissance, and is in part responsible for the new dualism which has arisen in our

175

education during the last century between culture and science.

Elsewhere, however, in all the great civilizations of the old world, religion and intellectual culture have been practically inseparable, because the tradition of civilization was also the tradition of a particular religion and the sacred books of that religion were the classics and basic matter of study for the whole educated class. Most of all is this the case in China, where from an early period the scholars took the place of the priests as the guardians of the sacred traditions of Chinese culture and where moral and intellectual and ritual culture were fused into an indissoluble unity.

All this, however, is only the external aspect of the problem, based on a very restricted sense of the term culture. What we are concerned with here is not literary culture but spiritual culture—the training of the mind in the way of the divine law. Some such process of spiritual discipline is implicit in the conception of human relations with superhuman reality which is the very essence of religion according to our definition. In the first place this involves the ritual discipline of approach by the correct formulas of prayer and ceremony. But in the second place it involves an inner discipline which renders the soul capable of transcending the ordinary level of humanity and makes it possible to attain superhuman experience and divine vision.

At first sight this would seem to lie outside the province of Natural Theology, since it represents precisely the element which is excluded by the traditional definition of the concept and reserved for the sphere of supernatural and revealed religion. But however this may be, there can be no doubt that every historical form of religion from the lowest to the highest (with the possible exception of Confucianism) does give a very important place to this interior discipline. Even on the lowest level of culture it is to be seen very clearly in the training of the Shaman who, as I have already shown, is one of the earliest and most universal figures in the history of religion. In my earlier chapter I was concerned with the Shaman mainly as a diviner and seer, the social organ of inspired utterance, but he is no less important as an ascetic and a " holy man " who has acquired by training the mastery of spiritual techniques.

From the earliest stages of culture we find the conviction that ascetic practices produce spiritual power and that they must normally be conducted according to the correct rules under the guidance of an experienced teacher. Thus the novice or pupil who has the vocation to become a Shaman has to undergo a far more rigorous and prolonged process of initiation than the ordinary man, since he has to face more formidable dangers—spiritual dangers. In North America the initiation of the Shaman and his quest for vision is ascetic. He prepares himself by fasting and penance, by prayer and solitude.

But in every part of the world it is also frequently associated with psychic abnormality. The Shaman is a man set apart by being different from other men. In Siberia especially, there is a general agreement that the Shaman is a highly neurotic type; it is only after a profound psychic crisis that he attains his professional status. He often suffers for years from illness or nervous affections. He loses his interest in ordinary affairs and ceases to share in the work or talk of his fellows. He goes out into the wilderness where he lies in trance and hears the voices of the spirits. The greater the Shaman the more painful is this process of " gathering power," so that among the Chuckchees they were often said to sweat blood. A great Yakut Shaman of the last century has described his experience in the following words—" When I was twenty years old I became very ill and began to see with my eyes and hear with my ears that which others did not see or hear. Nine years I

177

struggled with myself and I did not tell anyone what was happening to me, as I was afraid that people would not believe me and would make fun of me. At last I became so seriously ill that I was on the verge of death; but when I started to shamanize I became better; and even now when I do not shamanize for a long time I become ill."[1]

The highly individualistic character of the Shaman's vocation and his spiritual power obviously involves possibilities of social conflict. In fact no figure is more feared by primitive society than the evil Shaman or magician who uses his relations with the spiritual world for his private advantage against the interests of society. But the conflict is resolved by the belief that the man who transcends society and acquires superhuman powers is also the man who is best able to help his fellow men in their spiritual necessities. Thus to quote Sieroszcewski again, " The duties undertaken by the Shaman are not easy: the struggle which he has to carry on is dangerous. There exist traditions about Shamans who were carried away still living from the earth to the sky, about others killed by spirits or struck down at their first meeting with the powers whom they dared to call upon. The wizard who decides to carry on this struggle has not only material gain in view but the alleviation of the griefs of his fellow men; the wizard who has the vocation, the faith and the conviction, who undertakes his duty with ecstasy and negligence of personal danger, inspired by the high ideal of sacrifice, such a wizard always exerts an enormous influence over his audience. After having seen once or twice such a real Shaman, I understood the distinction that the natives drew between the ' Great ', the ' Middling ' and the ' Mocking ' or deceitful Shamans."[2]

[1] Czaplicka, *Aboriginal Siberia,* p. 173 from Sieroszcewski's *Twelve Years among the Yakuts* (1896).
[2] Czaplicka, *op. cit.,* 176 from Sieroszcewski, *op. cit.,* 639.

(ii)

The training of the Shaman with its spiritual dangers and hardships and its goal of supernatural knowledge and power, has a close analogy with the spiritual discipline of the ascetic " holy man " in the higher cultures. In India, especially, the tradition of asceticism is so ancient and deeply rooted that it carries us back to a point at which the two types are almost indistinguishable. In none of the archaic civilizations is the ritual learning of the priestly class more closely associated with the ideal of individual acquisition of supernatural power by ascetic practices. And the link between the two is focused in the characteristic Indian institution of the *Vanaprasthas*, the ascetics who retire to the jungle to study the inner meaning of the sacrificial rites and formulas. From the moment when meditation on the ritual becomes more important than the rite itself, the ascetic becomes more important than the priest and the inner way of enlightenment and perfection more important than the ritual order.

We have seen how this spiritual revolution was accomplished in the early Upanishads, and thenceforward all the great Indian religions and religious philosophies are disciplines of salvation essentially concerned with the quest for individual enlightenment and perfection. But this quest for salvation involves a similar conflict between the social ideals of the old theocratic order and the anti-social individualism of the pure ascetic that we have already noted in the case of the Shaman. But the conflict is now transposed to a transcendental and metaphysical plane. Nowhere in fact do we find such a radical questioning and negation of the whole social-cultural scale of values as in the great creative age of Indian religious thought. As an illustration of this I will quote the story which forms the introduction of the *Maitrayana Upanishad*, since it gives a singularly forcible statement of the fundamental psychological attitude that inspires the whole movement of world renunciation and world transcendence.

" A king, named Brihadratha, having established his son in his sovereignty, went into the forest, because he considered this body as transient, and had obtained freedom from all desires. Having performed the highest penance, he stands there, with uplifted arms, looking up to the sun. At the end of a thousand days, the Saint Sakayanya, who knew the Self, came near, burning with splendour, like a fire without smoke. He said to the king: ' Rise, rise! Choose a boon! '

" The King, bowing before him, said: ' O Saint, I know not the Self, thou knowest the essence [of the Self]. We have heard so. Teach it us.'

" Sakayanya replied: ' This was achieved of yore; but what thou askest is difficult to obtain. O Aikshvaka, choose other pleasures.'

" The King, touching the Saint's feet with his head, recited this Gatha:

" ' O Saint, what is the use of the enjoyment of pleasures in this offensive, pithless body—a mere mass of bones, skin, sinews, marrow, flesh, seed, blood, mucus, tears, phlegm, ordure, water, bile, and slime! What is the use of the enjoyment of pleasures in this body which is assailed by lust, hatred, greed, delusion, fear, anguish, jealousy, separation from what is loved, union with what is not loved, hunger, thirst, old age, death, illness, grief, and other evils.

" 'And we see that all this is perishable, as these flies, gnats, and other insects, as herbs and trees, growing and decaying. And what of these? There are the great ones, mighty wielders of bows, rulers of empires, and kings and others, who before the eyes of their whole family surrendered the greatest happiness, and passed on from this world to that. And what of these? There are other great ones. We have seen the destruction of supernatural beings, demons and demigods, ghosts and goblins, snakes and vampires. And what of these? There is the drying up of the great oceans, the falling of mountains, the moving of the pole-star, the cutting of the wind-ropes (that hold the stars), the submergence of the earth, and the departure of the gods from their place. In such a world as this, what is the use of the enjoyment of pleasures, if he who has fed on them is seen to return (to this world) again and again! Deign therefore to take me out! In this world I am like a frog in a dry well. O Saint, thou art my way, thou art my way.' "[1]

However alien all this may be from modern Western views of life and of religion, we must admit that it represents, in an extreme and paradoxical form, an experience that is fundamental in the natural religious experience of mankind. No doubt it is worlds away from the social conformism of Confucius or from the Hellenic idealization of nature, but it is more characteristically religious than either of them.

And in both these cases, the absence of this world-renouncing element is emphasized and compensated by the existence of an undercurrent of ideas and religious practices which resemble the Indian disciplines of salvation. Thus in China there is the ancient Taoist tradition which is mystical and unsocial and centres in the figure of the wonder-working hermit saint; and in Greece we have the Orphic tradition which was also a discipline of salvation and a path of liberation, and had a real though obscure influence on the ideals of Greek philosophy from Pythagoras and Empedocles to the Neo-Platonists.

[1] Maitrayana Upanishad I, 2–4 (S.B.E. XV, 287–90).

II

India, however, provides the classical example of this aspect of religious development and it is there that we can best study the influence of the interior discipline of spiritual perfection and the ideal of world renunciation on culture and the order of society, since it is only in India that these conceptions acquired an unchallenged domination for thousands of years over the whole life and thought of a great independent culture.

Now the peculiar character of the Indian development is due above all to the doctrine of the transmigration of the soul from body to body and from existence to existence and to the ideas of retribution (Karma) and release (Moksha) that were associated with it. This belief is found in one form or another in a large number of primitive cultures, but it does not appear in the earliest religious literature of India—in the Rig Veda—and it finds its first clear expression in the earlier Upanishads. From that time forward, however, it obsessed the mind of India. The prospect of the endless cycle of births and deaths generated a feeling of horror and repulsion as strong as the Puritan fear of hell, and made the desire for final release the dominant motive of the religious quest.

No doubt there must have been a large body of orthodox opinion which was mainly concerned with the fulfilment of the ritual law and with ensuring that proper provision was made for the souls of the ancestors, in the appointed way of sacrifice and Shradda or Oblation. But the philosophers and the religious leaders were more and more concerned with the one problem, how to secure release from the chain of rebirth which was also the law of retribution, and from them this preoccupation penetrated more and more deeply into the heart of Indian religion.

Once granted the continuity of the chain of existences, which was accepted by the Indian as a self-evident fact,[1] the various methods or " paths " which were adopted in order to transcend or end the process possess a strictly rational character. This is true even of asceticism itself, since the conquest of the body and the renunciation of all physical satisfaction is the most simple and obvious way to free the soul from the attachment to bodily existence. At its crudest this method may take the form of voluntary suicide as in the case of the Jains who regard death by starvation (like the Albigensian practice of *endura*) as the crown of the religious life.

But the Indian mind was not satisfied with this *simpliste* solution. It was felt from the beginning that external methods could only produce external results and that the true deliverance must be a spiritual one and achieved by spiritual means. But the true spiritual way is the way of knowledge or metaphysical intuition, *Vidya*. For the man who has attained knowledge—who has realized the supreme truth of the identity of his consciousness with the Absolute Spirit, there is no return. He is freed by his vision from the chain of existence. Death and birth no longer have power over him. He is one with the Brahman-Atman.

This is the classical solution of the great Upanishads which has remained definitive for orthodox Indian thought and philosophy ever since. It does not, however, exclude the validity or indeed the necessity of moral discipline and ascetic practices as preparatory stages towards the goal of perfection. In this way the psychological asceticism of Yoga which consists of specialized techniques for gaining complete mastery over

[1] " So far as I remember there has seldom been before or after Buddha any serious attempt to prove or disprove the doctrine of rebirth. All schools of philosophy except the Carvakas believed in it and so little is known of the Carvaka Sutras that it is difficult to say what they did to refute this doctrine. The Buddha also accepts it as a fact and does not criticize it." S. Dasgupta, *History of Indian Philosophy*, I, 87.

mind and body and producing states of autohypnosis and trance is a natural auxiliary method to the more purely metaphysical discipline of the Upanishads and the Vedanta.

Hence it was not the ascetics who were responsible for the most powerful criticism of the way of knowledge and the orthodox Brahmin philosophy of religion. The great challenge to Brahminism both as a Way of Works or Ritual Action and as a Way of Knowledge or Metaphysical Intuition proceeded from the ethical rationalism of Buddhism, the second of the great world religions that India has produced.

Now Buddhism is the most perfect example of what has been called a discipline of salvation, since it was even more obsessed with the problem of rebirth and more exclusively and systematically concentrated on the search for deliverance than all the other schools and philosophies. " As the ocean has but one taste—the taste of salt," says the Buddha, " so also my Law and Discipline have but one savour, the savour of Deliverance."[1] Early Buddhist doctrine is marked by a severely practical and rational spirit which is very unlike that of the Brahmanas or the Upanishads. It demands no extremes of asceticism, it promises no revelation of divine mysteries. Everything is brought down to a few very simple truths—suffering and the cause of suffering; the extinction of suffering and the way to the extinction of suffering. These are the Four Noble Truths on which the Way is founded. There is no knowledge beyond these truths and no reality outside this way. The whole of religion, the whole of philosophy and the whole of human life are reduced to the interior way of moral and mental discipline, by which the nothingness of existence is realized and the extinction of desire and passion is attained.

How is it possible to reconcile this extremity of introversion and negation with the existence of culture and the order of

[1] *Chulla Vagga*, IX, 1–4.

social life? We have the undoubted record of history, engraved for all time on rocks and pillars, that it was actually accepted conscientiously and intelligently as a principle of government by the greatest ruler India has ever known—Asoka, the founder of the Maurya Empire, who became a convert to Buddhism c. 260 B.C.

And even apart from that, the records of Buddhist monasticism prove that the moral law of the Buddha has justified itself through the ages as a positive social force which has exercised an even greater direct influence on the civilization of Southern, Eastern and Central Asia than orthodox Brahmanism has done.

Nor is it difficult to see why this should have been the case, since any effective spiritual discipline that is inspired by high moral ideals must inevitably be a powerful social force. The problem is rather how a religious doctrine which is so lacking in positive theological beliefs and so negative and pessimistic in its attitude to human life can provide the motive power necessary for effective moral action.

The answer seems to be that Buddhism contains a much larger element of positive religion than its philosophy seems to suggest. In the first place even though the Buddhist discipline of salvation is a *via negativa*, it remains a discipline of salvation —a religious absolute; and even though it admits no worship of gods and no divine order of nature, the way of salvation is itself divine; inasmuch as it is the way to an absolute good which transcends human life and human knowledge.

However negative are the terms of definition, the goal, spiritual perfection, is a transcendent religious object capable of inspiring religious emotion and moral action.

And in the second place the figure of the Buddha—the Enlightened One who has pity on men and opens to them a pathway of deliverance from evil—is an object of religious devotion and religious worship. Buddha may not be god in the theological sense, but he is a much higher and more spiritual figure than the gods of the Indian pantheon who are the official objects of prayer and sacrifice. Buddhism never denied the gods—there were gods and demigods, devils and goblins, dragons and vampires—there was room and to spare for all of them in the infinite series of worlds and heavens and hells in which Indian cosmology ran riot. But all these beings, good and bad, high and low, pitiful and terrible, were alike bound to the wheel of existence and to the law of retribution from which the Buddha alone had found the way of salvation and release.

The delightful story in the Dialogues of the Buddha concerning the monk who indulged in cosmological enquiries shows the fundamental scepticism of the Buddhists towards the mythology they had transcended. The monk, who desired to know where the world ends, made a tour of enquiry among the gods and the successive heavens and the gods replied: " We do not know, O monk, where the world ends. But there is Brahma, the great Brahma, the creator of all things, he will know the answer." So when the monk at last found himself in the presence of Brahma he asked him where the world ends. And Brahma answered: " I am the Great Brahma, the supreme one, the mighty, the all-seeing, the ruler, the lord of all, the creator, the chief of all, appointing to each his place, the father of all that are or that are to be." " I do not ask you, friend," said the monk, " whether you are indeed all that you say. But I ask you where the four elements cease, leaving no trace behind." Then the great Brahma took the monk by the arm and led him aside and said, " These gods my servants hold me to be such that there is nothing I cannot see, understand, realize. Therefore I gave no answer in their presence. But I do not really know where the world ends. Go you now, return to the Lord, ask him the question and accept the answer according as he shall make reply."[1]

And the answer of Buddha was always the same as that of the mediaeval Christian monk. A man must not busy himself in vain questions that do not concern him. Let him concern himself with the way of perfection and the salvation of his soul, for these are the only things that matter.

But if the Buddha is the saviour and the gateway to eternal deliverance, he is for all practical purposes God; and with the rise of the Mahayana system in the first centuries of the Christian era, Buddhism formally accepted this conclusion and worshipped the Buddha under divine titles similar to those which the Great Brahma had claimed for himself in the story I have just quoted: " The Father of the World, the Self-Born, the Healer, the Protector of All Creatures." Thus the Mahayana which dominates the historic development of Buddhism in China and Central Asia has become as theistic as or more theistic than Brahmanism itself, being inspired by a passionate personal devotion to the Saviour Gods who were the Buddhas. Thus the primitive Buddhist discipline of salvation has been transformed into a way of devotion directed to the worship of the Buddha and the salvation of man and all other creatures. The sober self-discipline of the old Buddhist monasticism has given place to an ethic of self-sacrifice and universal love which finds expression in the Bodhicharyavatara of Santideva, a poem which expresses all that is noblest and purest in Buddhist spirituality.

This transformation of Buddhism appears to have taken place in the Kushan empire which extended from Oxus to the Jumna and which formed the main channel through which the new religion was diffused in Turkestan and China. It is there-

[1] *Dialogues of the Buddha*, tr. Rhys Davids, I, 280.

for possible, even probable, that it represents a fusion of Indian and Iranian religious influences, such as one would expect in a culture of mixed origins. But we also find a similar transformation taking place in Hinduism at the same time, if, as many scholars believe, the Bhagavad Gita dates from this period. For in the Gita we see the same transformation of the way of knowledge into the way of devotion and the same transition from an impersonal metaphysical doctrine to a personal theistic faith. Moreover the God of the Gita like the Buddha of the Mahayana is a Saviour God who manifests himself on earth for the salvation of man.

" For whensoever the Law fails and lawlessness uprises, then do I bring myself to bodied birth.

" To guard the righteous, to destroy evil doers, to establish the Law, I come unto birth age after age. . . ."

" Father of the universe am I, mother, ordainer, grandsire, the thing that is known and the being that makes clean, the word OM, the Rik, the Sama, and the Yajus.

" The Way, the Supporter, the Lord, the Witness, the Dwelling, the Refuge, the Friend, the Origin, the Dissolution, the abiding place, the house of ward, the changeless Seed."[1]

But this personal devotion to a divine saviour is united alike in the Gita and in the Mahayana with the ideal of spiritual perfection, the exercise of virtue and the cultivation of the interior life. In the Mahayana this represents the continuity of the old Buddhist tradition, whereas in the Gita it is expressed in Yoga terminology. But in addition to these two elements the Gita adds a third principle which is the *raison d'être* of the poem and which has been of immense importance for the religious life of India. This is the doctrine that a man can win salvation only by pursuing the duties of his state and caste in a spirit of disinterested devotion. The warrior need not

[1] *Bhagavad Gita*, tr. Barnett, IV, 7–8, IX, 17–18.

become a monk or a hermit in order to be a saint, the true path of perfection is the performance of a man's social duty without attachment to the fruits of his action. In this way the metaphysical absolutism of the Upanishads and the monastic ideal of individual perfection are reconciled with cultural values and with the claims of the social order.

Nevertheless this reconciliation is not complete nor is it altogether satisfying from the moral point of view, since it involves the uncritical acceptance of the whole ritual and social law as embodied in the caste system. Moreover it is not inspired by the moral doctrine and example of a great historical teacher like Buddha; it is worked into a mythical episode in the heroic epic, which is rather as though Plato had put the arguments of the *Phaedo* into the mouth of one of the Homeric heroes and incorporated them in the Iliad.

Hence the Gita in spite of its immense popularity and influence has not changed the religious ideal of India. Arjuna, the happy warrior, the hero of the Gita, who attains salvation by the performance of his duty in battle has never displaced the figure of the world-renouncing ascetic and contemplative as the pattern of Indian sanctity.

And the same is true of Buddhism where the new Mahayana ideal of devotion to the salvation of others did not displace the older way of moral asceticism and individual self-perfection as the dominant religious motive. Indeed, in the development of Northern Buddhism the Dhyana (Zen) school of contemplation or mystical intuition which has been so important in mediaeval China and modern Japan approximates to the antinomian quietism of the Taoists and this represents a deviation from primitive Buddhism in the opposite direction from that of the moral activism of the Bodhisatva ideal.

The Western student of Eastern religion and especially of Mahayana Buddhism is apt to be oppressed and bewildered by the tropical luxuriance of its development. He is lost in a jungle of metaphysical systems and sacred literatures which have become inextricably interwoven in the course of ages, so that in spite of the immense spiritual energy that has been expended, he is often brought back to the point from which he set out without any clear knowledge of what has been achieved.

Nevertheless, underlying all this complex development there is a unity of religious experience which is no less striking than the unity in diversity which characterizes the conception of the ritual order in the different archaic civilizations. This unity is the conviction that the true end of the religious life is to be found within the soul itself and is reached by a psychological process of introversion and concentration. This interior way of perfection begins with asceticism and moral discipline, proceeds by contemplation and enlightenment, and culminates in the experience of divine union or identity in which all distinctions are transcended and the soul is merged in eternal and absolute Being. This experience may be started in either theistic or pantheistic terms as in the Upanishads and the Gita, in Sankara and Ramanuja, and in the various schools of Mahayana Buddhism. It is however always a *via negativa*, a search for the Absolute by the denial or stripping away of all forms and images, and the whole positive content of consciousness. And the result of this process can only be expressed in negative terms, " Neti Neti " (" Not so, Not so"). It is called *Moksha*: deliverance; cessation (*Nirvana*); the void (*Sunyata*); isolation (*Kaivalya*).

It is in fact the negative intuition of transcendence which I have described in my second chapter, developed systematically as the principle of a process of spiritual integration and as the goal of the religious life.

Is it then possible to maintain that what is known in the West as mysticism is as much a part of Natural Theology as the belief in the moral law and the law of nature? If prayer is natural to man, there is no reason to reject the evidence that the movement of introversion and concentration by which the soul seeks the way to a transcendent absolute reality in its own depths is not peculiar to a single religion or a single cultural tradition but is a universal form of religious experience. No doubt it is in India that this experience has achieved its classical expressions and has influenced religion most deeply. But it has never been confined to India. It is to be found from Europe to Japan and from North Africa to Mongolia. It is approximately conterminous with the higher cultures and with the world religions, and reached its highest development in the periods when the civilization of the Old World was most intellectually and artistically productive.

What then is its relation to culture? How is it possible to reconcile the negative world-renouncing character of this form of religion with the positive aims and the social activity of an advanced civilization?

In fact the follower of these religious ideals would maintain that the true culture is the cultivation of the soul—the discipline of salvation—and what modern Westerns call culture is merely the outward shell—the garment of works—which the soul has secreted as a protective covering like the shell of an oyster.

Or in a less extreme form, it might be said that culture is the necessary social discipline which subserves the higher ends of the spiritual life. This is the thesis which is familiar to us in the West in its Platonic, Aristotelian and scholastic forms and which occupies an important place in the theodicy of St. Thomas—notably in the Third Book of the *Contra Gentiles*. " True happiness," he argues, " does not consist in physical or social goods, or in moral virtues. The final good of man is to be found only in the contemplation of God and it is to this act that all human activities seem to be directed as their last end." For this, health of body is necessary, and all artificial necessaries of life are means to health. Freedom from passion is necessary, and this is secured by prudence and the moral virtues. Freedom from external troubles is necessary, and this is the purpose of the whole order of social life and government. " And so, if things are considered aright, it will be seen that all human states and occupations (officia) serve as means to the contemplation of truth."[1]

This conception of the order of culture as a preparation to the order of contemplation or scale of ascent to it, is the classical theory that is common to the great world religions. It is developed particularly strongly by orthodox Hinduism, as expressed for example in the Gita, where the caste system provides for the integration of the social and spiritual hierarchies. Nevertheless elsewhere in Hinduism and to an even greater degree in Buddhism there remains a certain unresolved dualism between the drastic world negation of the contemplative and the moral and social discipline of the order of culture. This dualism finds expression in China and Japan in the co-existence of two distinct and contradictory religions within a single society—the contemplative religion of the Buddhist and Taoist monk who disregards social ties and social obligations, and the social ethics of the Confucian scholar who denies or sets aside the absolute claim of pure transcendent religion.

And elsewhere we find the co-existence of two contradictory attitudes within the same religion as in the Buddhism of Southern and South Eastern Asia, where there is no vital religious connection between the monastic ideal of contemplative perfection and the semi-pagan worship of the spirits of nature which is the working religion of the common people. Instead of the popular religion being spiritualized by the contemplative ideal, there is a tendency for the higher religion

[1] D. Thom. *Cont. Gen.*, III, xxxvii.

to be invaded and contaminated by the subrational forces of the pagan underworld as in Tantric Buddhism and in some forms of sectarian Hinduism.

For in religions of pure contemplation there is the danger of a divorce from historical reality and from the social order which deprives it of spiritual efficacy and creativity in the order of culture. The great verse of the Pragnaparamita Sutra, " The verse of the great wisdom, the unsurpassed verse, the verse that extinguishes all pain " is also the epitaph on Buddhism as a living and creative religion:

" O Wisdom gone away, gone, gone to the other shore, landed on the other shore, Svaha."

In the first chapter I said that religion was like a bridge between two worlds by means of which the order of culture is brought into conscious relation with the transcendent reality of spiritual being. But in these religions of negation and pure contemplation, the bridge is open in only one direction. It is a way of escape from the city into the wilderness and the spirit that goes out does not return again. Thus the world of culture is gradually weakened and finally deserted, like the great Buddhist cities of ancient Ceylon where the jungle has returned and swallowed up palaces and monasteries and irrigation tanks, leaving only the figure of Buddha contemplating the vanity of action and the cessation of existence.

CHAPTER X

Religion and Cultural Change

RARITY of pure cultures. Possibilities of internal conflict implicit in the nature of mixed cultures. A high cultural achievement usually involves a synthesis of different cultural traditions. Relative instability of such achievements owing to the tension of diverse elements. Function of religion as a unifying force in times of cultural synthesis and as a revolutionary force in times of cultural disintegration. If religion is too deeply committed to a particular cultural synthesis, it fails to maintain its transcendent character. On the other hand, if religion attempts to emancipate itself completely from its bond with culture, it makes for the secularization of culture. Neither alternative satisfactory from the religious point of view, but the former is often imposed by social authority. Necessity for the vital collaboration of religion and culture. Conditions of such a collaboration. The ideal of the spiritual integration of culture.

CHAPTER X

Religion and Cultural Change

I

WE HAVE seen that every social culture is at once a material way of life and a spiritual order. Culture as a common way of life is inseparable from culture as a common tradition of language and thought and a common inheritance of knowledge, and this in turn involves an organized attempt to co-ordinate human action with the transcendent divine power which rules the world and on which man's life depends.

In the typical cultures to which I have so often referred —the culture of ancient Egypt or ancient China, the Pueblo culture of New Mexico, and so on—the material and spiritual factors interpenetrate one another so completely that they form an inseparable unity, so that religion and life have become one. Every moment of life, every social occasion, every gesture and form of expression is consecrated by religious tradition and invested with religious significance. From the peasant in the field and the craftsman in his workshop to the priest in his temple and Pharaoh on his throne, the whole society obeys the same laws, moves with the same rhythm, breathes the same spirit. The gods are the life of the land, and human life follows the pattern of the divine ritual. In an extreme case, like the Maya culture, it is even possible that the life of the state obeys the requirements of the sacred order to such a degree that the otherwise inexplicable abandonment of the great temple cities may have been dictated by the determination of a ritual cycle.

But pure typical cultures of this kind are comparatively rare. In the majority of cases a culture represents a fusion of a number of different elements, and the history of world civilization is a complex process of diffusion and cross-fertilization and hybridization like the blending of different racial elements in the growth of a nation. In fact the two processes are often difficult to distinguish, since the most common form of cultural change is that which results from the conquest of one people by another, so that it also involves biological and racial changes.

A remarkable example of this two-fold process is to be seen in the Northern Bantu states of Central Africa—Unyoro, Ankole, Ruanda and Uganda—where a conquering people of Hamitic race and pastoral culture have superimposed themselves on a subject population of negro agriculturists.

In the East, in Uganda proper, any racial distinction has long since disappeared, though the form of the state and the institution of kingship are the same in both areas. But in the western parts of this region, the racial distinction is still clear cut, between the tall warrior nobles—the Bahima—who live on the products of their herds, and the short peasant serfs—the Bairo—who live on the fruits of the earth. Accordingly there has developed a rudimentary but clearly defined caste system which is based on marriage restrictions and food tabus, as well as on social and political privileges.

It is obvious that such a situation involves infinite possibilities of cultural conflict. Actually they are limited by the extreme simplicity of the elements involved. The institution of kingship provides the necessary bond of union between the different classes, and since the royal harem is recruited indifferently from every element in the population, the dynasty tends—except in Ruanda—to be a less pure representation of the ruling race than the aristocracy. Moreover in Ankole, at least, the state cult of Bagyendwana, the royal drums, which are the national fetish or palladium, transcends the distinction of classes and castes. The serfs as well as the nobles can bring their offerings to Bagyendwana and appeal to it for justice. For all the peoples of Ankole are " the children of Bagyendwana " " who is like the king only greater. For the king is the servant of Bagyendwana ".[1]

Thus the exaltation of the office of kingship and the religious cult associated with it seem sufficient to maintain the stability and coherence of these heterogeneous elements.

But in proportion as the cultural elements involved are deeper and more self-conscious, this becomes more difficult; as we see in India where the thousandfold complexity of the caste system represents an elaborate defence-mechanism to safeguard the purity of a cultural tradition.

But even so, what is defended is itself by no means an un-mixed culture, if, as seems probable, the main stream of Indian culture has its origin in a synthesis or syncretism of a highly advanced autochthonous culture with the tradition and language of chariot-driving, cattle-herding warriors from Central Asia. If that is the case, we should interpret the rise of the classical Indian systems of thought and social organization as due to the reassertion of the submerged elements of the archaic Indian culture against the warrior culture of the Aryan invaders. Unfortunately the historical evidence for this process of syncretism is lacking and we can only hazard a guess that the classical Indian spiritual attitude of world-renunciation and the quest for Nirvana had its social background in the profound divergence of two alien and incommunicable ways of life which, so to speak, cancelled one another out.

[1] K. Oberg, *The Kingdom of Ankole in Uganda* in *African Political Systems*, ed. M. Fortes and E. E. Evans Pritchard, pp. 150-7 (1940).

But however this may be, there is abundant evidence to prove that no type of social change is more common, or more profound in its effect on culture, than the reaction of an urban or peasant culture of the archaic type against the warrior culture that has subjugated it. Again and again we see in history how the power of the " gods of the land " reasserts itself, even when the native population has been subjugated and has lost its identity as a people.

We see it in ancient Greece where the old chthonic cults and deities of the pre-Hellenic Mediterranean world survive side by side with the gods of Olympus.

We see it in a still more sharply defined form in the age-long spiritual struggle of the Hebrew worshippers of Jehovah from the desert against the subtle and pervasive influence of the native Canaanite religion.

In many cases, however, there is no open conflict, but a gradual and almost unconscious adjustment and symbiosis of the different ways of life. The warrior noble and the peasant serf each lives his own life and follows his own tradition without religious conflict, and there ensues a gradual process of social and spiritual interpenetration, out of which after centuries a new integration of culture emerges. The great ages of cultural achievement represent as a rule the culmination of some such process of spiritual fusion, and it is in the sphere of religion that the new synthesis finds its characteristic expression. This does not involve the emergence of a new religion, but rather the reinterpretation of an existing religious tradition through new cultural forms—which thus acquire a classical character that endures, as long as the particular culture survives.

II

We can study this process in detail in our own civilization in the case of the synthesis in which mediaeval culture attained its classical form.

The main elements of this synthesis had been in contact with one another for 700 years, but it was not until the twelfth and thirteenth centuries that the process of interpenetration and fusion had gone far enough to produce the wonderful flowering of culture and institutions which deserves the name of the mediaeval renaissance.

This age the saw creation of Gothic architecture; the achievement of the intellectual synthesis of Christian Aristotelianism; the rise of the universities, the communes and the free cities; the development of representative institutions and the system of Estates; the rise of new vernacular literature, and a new type of lyrical poetry; the institution of chivalry; the creation of new types of religious orders, and the Franciscan movement with its cult of voluntary poverty. In all these diverse manifestations of culture, religion had a part—whether as a directly creative and inspiring force, or as consecrating and ennobling institutions like knighthood which had their origin in secular needs.

Nevertheless although the mediaeval synthesis appeared to achieve complete cultural unity and to embrace every aspect of social and intellectual life, it was in fact highly unstable and began to show signs of tension and internal conflict from the moment it was completed; as we can see in the poem of Dante which is at once the supreme literary expression of the mediaeval synthesis and a prophetic denunciation of the apostasy of Christendom.

In fact it was little more than three centuries after the

flowering of the mediaeval " Gothic " culture, that Western culture experienced the revolutionary changes of the Reformation period which destroyed the religious and to some extent the cultural unity of the mediaeval world.

Yet even here the revolt was not a revolt against religion but rather an explosion of dynamic religious forces against the synthesis which united the old religious tradition of Christendom with a particular complex of social institutions and ideological forms.

The whole process is an exceptionally clear example of the double rôle which religion plays in relation to culture, *i.e.* (*a*) as a unifying force in the creation of a cultural synthesis and (*b*) as a revolutionary disruptive force in times of social change.

And since these two rôles are more or less simultaneous, a complex culture is always a field of tension between opposing religious forces which are continually striving against one another.

To take a modern and familiar example; no historian can ignore the immense influence of the non-conformist churches and sects in England from the seventeenth to the nineteenth centuries, as channels for the new social forces which failed to find adequate recognition in the agrarian aristocratic society which was so closely identified with the Established Church. And these dissident religious movements were most active and vital at the very time when Anglicanism came nearest to achieving a form of cultural synthesis.

No doubt it is often difficult to trace any intelligible connection between the tenets of a particular sect and the interests or social constitution of a particular class. No historian, for example, has attempted to show why the yeoman farmers of north-west England in the later seventeenth century were drawn to the doctrines of non-resistance and the Inner Light, whereas the belief in the Fifth Monarchy and the temporal rule of the Saints Militant found support among very similar social types in other parts of England a generation earlier.

There is, no doubt, an accidental socio-political element in these divisions, such as that which determined that the East Syrians should be Nestorians, while their neighbours to the west, of the same race and language, adopted the diametrically opposite tenets of Monophysitism.

Nevertheless in many cases the relation between the social and religious factor seems clear enough, as in the appeal of the Methodist movement with its intense other-worldliness and emotionalism to the disinherited proletariat of eighteenth and early nineteenth century England or in the Congregationalism of early New England with its conviction of divine election and its aristocracy of grace.

It is easy to see why the revolutionary religious impulse which is the animating principle of all the great sectarian and minority movements should be characterized by a spirit of extreme other-worldliness and alienation from ordinary cultural values. What is more surprising is that this other-worldliness is usually combined with an exceptional degree of economic enterprise and great powers of social adaptability. This has often been noticed in connection with the development of the Protestant sects in western Europe and America, but it is equally characteristic of the very different type of sectarianism which existed in Tsarist Russia, where not only the Old Believers but also the adherents of the most extreme form of anti-social asceticism—the Skoptsy[1]—were often wealthy and successful merchants or money-changers. Moreover we find the same thing in the East, with the Armenians in

---

[1] A millenniarist sect which arose in Russia in the time of Catherine the Great and was characterized by the practice of castration, based on a literal interpretation of Matthew XIX, 12. An offshoot of the sect exists in Rumania where many of the cabdrivers in Bucharest used to belong to it.

Turkey, and in India in the case of the most ancient and unchanging of all religious minorities—the Jains.

Thus the social detachment which results from a spiritual alienation from the dominant culture and the religion that is associated with it does not necessarily produce social impotence or failure. For the detached elements acquire a greater degree of social fluidity which enables them to respond more easily to new needs and situations. On the other hand, they inevitably undermine the existing synthesis of religion and culture and tend, often unconsciously and unintentionally, towards the secularization of culture.

Often indeed the religious minority has its own cultural ideal, whether this looks forward to a revolutionary Utopia, like the Fifth Kingdom or the Age of the Spirit, or backwards towards an idealized traditional sacred order, like the Holy Russia of the Old Believers.

More rarely we find clear-sighted dissidents like Roger Williams in the seventeenth century, who take a radically secular view of the state and claim for the religious community only the same rights and independence as are possessed by any private association of merchants or craftsmen.

But in either case the practical effect is the same—the existing synthesis of religion and culture is discredited, the dynamic forces of religion are drawn away into new channels and what was yesterday an immemorial sacred order is seen as a dead weight of empty forms and superstitions which crushes down the human spirit.

As a rule the revolutionary criticism of a sectarian movement is directed not against the dominant culture itself but against the established orthodox religion which is thus made responsible for the social injustice and moral evils of the existing order. The prophetic condemnation of all existing forms of organized religion is indeed characteristic of this sectarian tendency. For example I quote the striking passage in George Fox's *Journal* which describes his spiritual experience when he lay all the winter at Enfield " warring in spirit with the evil spirits of the world ". " I was under great suffering at this time beyond what I have words to declare. For I was brought into the deep and saw all the religions of the world and people that lived in them and priests that held them up, who were as a company of men-eaters, eating up the people like bread and gnawing the flesh off their bones. But as for true religion and worship, and ministers of God, alack! I saw there was none among those of the world that pretended to it. For they that pretended to be the church were but a company of men-eaters, men of cruel visages and of long teeth; and though they had cried against the men-eaters in America, I saw they were in the same nature."[1]

It is obvious that such drastic and revolutionary criticisms must arouse equally violent movements of repression which are strongest where the bond between religion and society is felt to be most vital, as we see in the fierce persecution of the Quakers in the theocratic polity of New England from 1658 to 1661. In these conflicts, it is the most religious elements on both sides that suffer most and provide the chief casualties, so that periods of religious war and persecution prepare the way for indifferentism and the secularization of culture, as happened in seventeenth century England, or in Russia, where the martyrdom of Avvakum and the downfall of his orthodox persecutor Nikon were the prelude to the rise of Peter the Great and the introduction of Western secularized civilization into Orthodox Russia.[2]

[1] *Journal* (8th ed.), II, 132–3.
[2] The resistance of the traditionalists to the reform of the rites service books of the Russian Church by the Patriarch Nikon (1652–66) was led by the Archpriest Avvakum (1620–81) whose autobiography is one of the most original books in Russian literature. After more than 20 years of exile and suffering he was burnt alive in 1681, and in the same year his former persecutor, Nikon, who had been deposed and imprisoned in 1666, died also.

III

Any religious movement which adopts a purely critical and negative attitude to culture is therefore a force of destruction and disintegration which mobilizes against it the healthiest and most constructive elements in society—elements which can by no means be dismissed as worthless from the religious point of view. On the other hand, the identification of religion with the particular cultural synthesis which has been achieved at a definite point of time and space by the action of historical forces is fatal to the universal character of religious truth. It is indeed a kind of idolatry—the substitution of an image made by man for the eternal transcendent reality. If this identification is carried to its extreme conclusion, the marriage of religion and culture is equally fatal to either partner, since religion is so tied to the social order that it loses its spiritual character, and the free development of culture is restricted by the bonds of religious tradition until the social organism becomes as rigid and lifeless as a mummy.

In fact all the great archaic religion-cultures like those of Egypt and Mesopotamia failed to escape this fate, in spite of the inestimable services that they rendered to the cause of civilization.

All of them were idolatrous orders which ultimately became fossil relics of a dead past, like Ptolemaic Egypt, where an alien dynasty of Macedonian adventurers was worshipped under the old Pharaonic titles and were represented on the walls of the temples wearing the old insignia of the divine monarchy. Even contemporary classical writers, like Diodorus and Cicero, who were not usually very sensitive to the contacts and contrasts of culture could not help being impressed by the survival of this unchanging mysterious culture. " *Ut occulte latet*," says Cicero, " *ut tota recondita est* ". There has never been a more curious example of an artificial cultural synthesis than this, in which the ruler lived a double life as an enlightened Hellenistic prince, the patron of philosophers and men of science, and at the same time as the divine head of the ancient sacred order, worshipped by the priests as the living image of Amon, and praised for his devotion to the divine animals and the wealth he lavished on their mummies and their tombs.

The immense mausoleum of the dead Apis bulls at Sakkarah with its 3,000 tombs is an apt monument and symbol of a religion that becomes bound to the corpse of a dead culture; and we cannot wonder at the violence with which the world religions rejected and condemned the idolatry of the earth-bound religions of the archaic culture.

Nevertheless this reaction was often characterized by excesses which were equally injurious to religion as a social force. The condemnation of matter and the body as evil, the flight from nature and the world of sense, the denial of the reality of the world, and the value of the social order—all appear to make any real synthesis between religion and culture impossible.

It is true, as we saw in the case of Buddhism, that the world religions have had a much more positive influence on culture than one might have expected. Nevertheless it is difficult to believe that the nihilism and disgust at existence expressed in so much early Buddhist literature did not in the long run reduce the cultural activity and lower the social vitality of its adherents.

Even a world religion which has such a strong social and historical consciousness as Islam compares very unfavourably with the earlier religions of the Near East in its influence on material culture. For, as Sir William M. Ramsay used to insist so forcibly in his studies of the religions and cultures of Asia Minor, the depopulation of these lands of ancient culture, the decline in the fertility of the soil, the abandonment of irrigation and the victory of the desert over the sown land were closely related to religious changes, above all to the loss of the archaic piety towards the earth and the powers of nature which once held nature and society in harmony with one another in allegiance to a common divine law.

IV

How is this profound primitive intuition of the dependence of human life on the divine law to be separated from the idolatrous identification of God's law with the temporal conditions of a particular age and society, without being also separated from its vital connection with man's earthly, bodily existence and transferred to a plane of inhuman abstraction? That is the vital problem on the solution of which the possibility of an organic synthesis of religion and culture depends.

History shows that the vital collaboration of religion and culture has been the normal condition of human society from the beginning, and that even the religions which seek to escape from life to the eternal cessation of Nirvana are driven in spite of themselves to clothe themselves in cultural forms. Indeed a religion which begins by asserting the absolute transcendence of the spiritual order often ends by becoming completely fused with the old idolatrous nature worship which remains the effective basis of culture, so that the metaphysical discipline of salvation becomes a cul-de-sac in which the dynamic power of religion is lost.

What then are the conditions which made a fruitful co-operation between religion and culture possible? On the one hand, the assertion of the absolute transcendent spiritual claims of religion must not be interpreted as a denial of the limited, historically conditioned and temporal values of culture, and on the other the forms of a particular culture, even when they are inspired or consecrated by a religious ideal, must not be regarded as possessing universal religious validity.

Actually, it is very hard to find any example of a religious culture which does not fail in this respect. For apart from the cultures which are idolatrous in the sense that they identified their own forms with the divine image, there are still more which attribute to their way of life and their social tradition a universal moral or spiritual validity, so that in practice they are identified with the divine order and the moral law.

The result is that every conflict of cultures is seen as a conflict of different spiritual principles, in other words a conflict of religions; and it usually becomes such in fact since the differences of culture and social tradition tend to ally themselves with differences of religious doctrine. This is particularly obvious in the history of the great theological controversies which accompanied the break-up of the Roman Empire. Here the differences of social tradition between the dominant Roman Hellenistic culture and the submerged cultures of the oriental peoples found expression on a religious plane in abstruse theological disputes concerning the union of divinity and humanity in the person of the Divine Word—questions which appear entirely unrelated to the cultural and national divisions which separated the Byzantine Greeks from the Syrians, the Armenians and the Egyptians.

In the past attempts have often been made by rulers and empires to overcome this source of conflict by a process of religious syncretism by which the gods of subject peoples are adopted into the pantheon of the conquerors, retaining their own temples and priesthoods.

The coming of the world religions destroyed the possibility of this solution in its simple form. Nevertheless in the East where the world religions met one another against a background of older and more primitive cults, attempts were made to achieve a similar syncretism on the highest level of religious thought.

This tendency attains perhaps its finest expression in the inscription which was inscribed by Abu'l Fazl, the friend of the great Akbar,[1] on a temple in Kashmir:

" *O God, in every temple I see people that see thee, and in every language I hear spoken, people praise thee.*
Polytheism and Islam feel after thee.
Each religion says, ' Thou art one, without equal.'
If it be a mosque, people murmur the holy prayer; and if it be a Christian Church, people ring the bell from love to thee.
Sometimes I frequent the Christian cloister, and sometimes the mosque
But it is thou whom I seek from temple to temple.
Thy elect have no feelings with heresy or with orthodoxy: for neither of them stands behind the screen of thy truth.
Heresy to the heretic, and religion to the orthodox,
But the dust of the rose-petal belongs to the heart of the perfume-seller."

Nevertheless these noble lines must not blind us to the fact that the religion of Akbar, the *Din Ilahi*, was a purely artificial creation, designed to serve the interests of Akbar's imperial policy, and to glorify his name, and that it never became a living religion.

[1]The greatest of the Moghul emperors, who ruled India from 1556 to 1605. He founded an eclectic religion which was intended to unite Moslems and Hindus in a common royal religion. His aims and ideals were described by his friend and minister, Abu'l Fazl (1551–1602), in his *Ain i Akbari*—the Institutes of Akbar.

The verses quoted above are ascribed to Abu'l Fazl's brother, Faizi, the Persian poet.

V

Such attempts to create a syncretism of different religious traditions in the interests of cultural and political unity are by no means uncommon. But it is much more unusual to find any deliberate attempt to co-ordinate a number of different cultural traditions in a common religious unity. In so far as this has been achieved, it has been due to the unconscious forces of culture-contact and historical development.

Nevertheless it is on these lines, rather than by the way of religious syncretism that the true solution is to be found. For although the order of religion transcends the order of culture, every culture becomes religious in so far as it recognizes its dependence on this higher order and seeks to bring the social order into conformity with the divine law.

Thus every social way of life may be a way to God, so long as it recognizes its human limitations and does not attempt to force its particular historical values into the place of universal divine truths.

It is the traditional teaching of Natural Theology that the elements of religious truth are common to the human race and accessible to every rational creature—that the Divine Being is the transcendent end towards which all the different ways of life converge and the divine law the universal norm by which all the different patterns of human behaviour can be co-ordinated. And this has also been the teaching of the world religions, like Buddhism and Christianity and Islam, for though they all assert the necessity of a supernatural revelation, they regard it as transcending human culture and universal to all men and all peoples. Thus the great world religions of the past actually created spiritual unities which transcended the limits of culture and brought together peoples of diverse origin

211

and alien ways of life—Indians and Thibetans, Greeks and Abyssinians, Latins and Scandinavians, Arabs and Malays and negroes—in common allegiance to a spiritual law and an eternal truth.

But this ideal of universal spiritual unity was never completely realized. For in the first place the underlying conflicts of culture and social tradition were always liable to reappear in the shape of a religious schism or sect. And secondly the world religions were mutually exclusive, each denying the claims of the other to spiritual universality and access to transcendent reality. In this way the world religions became each the spiritual principle of a separate culture or superculture, so that almost down to our own times civilized humanity has been divided between five or six different religion-cultures (if I may use the expression) each of which was a closed world, far more remote from the rest than the pre-historic religion-cultures when the archaic culture was diffused from one end of the old world to the other.

VI

But in our own age and during the last two centuries a great revolution has taken place which has entirely transformed the situation. The barriers of the closed religion-cultures have fallen and for the first time in history the world in its physical entirety has become one.

This revolutionary movement had its source in Western culture and up to a point it may be viewed as the progressive expansion of this particular culture. It found its ideological basis in the philosophy of the eighteenth century Enlightenment which, as we have seen, represents the final phase of the humanist Natural Theology.

But the tendency to identify modern Western culture with civilization in the absolute sense was not confined to the men of the Enlightenment.

Indeed its classical expression is to be found in the writings of Cardinal Newman who was the life-long adversary of Liberalism and rationalism. In his *Idea of a University* he writes as follows, " Considering, then, the characteristics of this great civilized Society . . . I think it has a claim to be considered as the representative Society and Civilization of the human race, as its perfect result and limit, in fact, those portions of the race which do not coalesce with it being left to stand by themselves as anomalies, unaccountable indeed, but for that very reason not interfering with what on the contrary has been turned to account and has grown into a whole. I call then this commonwealth pre-eminently and emphatically Human Society, and its intellect the Human Mind, and its decisions the sense of mankind, and its disciplined and cultivated state Civilization in the abstract, and the territory on which it lies the *orbis terrarum,* or the World."[1]

In was in this spirit of sublime unquestioning certitude that modern Western civilization set out to conquer the world in the eighteenth and nineteenth centuries. And though this certitude has disappeared, and the ideology on which it was founded has lost its appeal (except perhaps in the U.S.A.), the process of social and economic unification which it generated still continues with undiminished intensity. The emphasis to-day however is no longer on Western ideas but rather on the Western scientific techniques which provide the common framework of human existence and on the basis of which a new scientific world civilization is being formed.

What is the situation of religion and in particular of the five great world religions in this new world that is unified,

[1] *Idea of a University,* p. 253–4.

organized and controlled by scientific knowledge and techniques? All of them survive and continue to influence human life, but all of them have lost their organic relation to society which was expressed in the traditional synthesis of religion and culture in East and West alike.

These fixed traditional orders were obstacles which had to be removed before the scientific revolution could be accomplished. Sometimes they were dissolved from within by ideological forces, sometimes from without by the guns of Western men-of-war and the conquests of European armies; and perhaps even more generally by a combination of both factors taking the form of civil war and political revolution.

Thus the scientific revolution has been almost inseparable from movements of social and political revolution and with a far-reaching secularization of social life which produces a new type of conflict between religion and culture. We see a typical example of this in the Russian Revolution and the twenty years of acute anti-religious conflict which followed it, but this instance is far from being unique, since we see the same process at work in the French Revolution and in many of the European revolutions of the nineteenth century, as well as in the twentieth century revolutions in Turkey and China. The result of these tendencies has been to produce a wider, more intense and more complete secularization of culture than the world has ever known.

For the new scientific culture is devoid of all positive spiritual content. It is an immense complex of techniques and specialisms without a guiding spirit, with no basis of common moral values, with no unifying spiritual aim. This was not evident so long as modern science was confined to the peoples of the West and maintained its connection with the ideology of Humanism and liberalism, but now that it has become truly world-wide, its spiritual neutrality or vacuity has become evident, since it can be taken over *en bloc* by any state which is able to train specialists and buy machinery and equipment, as Japan has done in the last sixty years.

A culture of this kind is no culture at all in the traditional sense—that is to say it is not an order which integrates every side of human life in a living spiritual community.

Indeed it may become the enemy of human life itself and the victory of technocracy may mean the destruction of humanity since it is impossible to ignore the way in which the latest triumphs of applied science have been turned to destructive ends.

VII

The events of the last few years portend either the end of human history or a turning point in it. They have warned us in letters of fire that our civilization has been tried in the balance and found wanting—that there is an absolute limit to the progress that can be achieved by the perfectionment of scientific techniques detached from spiritual aims and moral values.

There are many, as for example H. G. Wells in his last days, who have drawn the extreme conclusion and believe that the process of disintegration that threatens the existence of civilization cannot be arrested or diverted.

If there were no alternative to the total secularization of culture, this pessimism would be justified.

But if, on the other hand, the movement of secularization represents only one aspect of human life—if mankind possesses other resources which have been temporarily neglected but which still remain available—it is possible to see the present situation as a temporary crisis due to over-secularization in a particular direction, which will be corrected by a swing of the pendulum in the opposite direction. This movement of alternation has always been part of the normal development of culture, and the recent movement of secularization is unique only in its extent and in the immensity of the forces it has generated. But there is no reason to believe that it will not ultimately be succeeded by a movement in the other direction towards religious belief and spiritual integration, as has been the case with all the more limited movements towards secularization and the disintegration of the synthesis between religion and culture in the past.

Religion is still a living force in the world to-day. No doubt it is difficult to estimate the hold religion possesses over men's minds and lives, for it is not a force which can easily be measured by statistical methods.

There are authorities like Professor Latourette who assert that so far as Christianity is concerned, the last century and a half have seen its widest expansion and its largest effect upon the human race.

There are others who argue that this advance has been superficial and peripheral, and that religion has lost more by the secularization of culture than it has gained by internal organization and missionary activity. However this may be, there can be no question that, on the one hand, it survives and in certain respects flourishes, and on the other hand that it has lost the organic relations with culture which it possessed in the great religion-cultures of antiquity and the Middle Ages.

Thus we have a secularized scientific world culture which is a body without a soul; while on the other hand religion maintains its separate existence as a spirit without a body.

This situation was tolerable as long as secular culture was dominated by the old liberal humanist ideology which had an intelligible relation with the Western Christian tradition, but it becomes unendurable as soon as this connection is lost and the destructive implications of a completely secularized order have been made plain.

We are faced with a spiritual conflict of the most acute kind, a sort of social schizophrenia which divides the soul of society between a non-moral will to power served by inhuman techniques and a religious faith and a moral idealism which have no power to influence human life. There must be a return to unity—a spiritual integration of culture—if mankind is to survive.

The whole history of culture shows that man has a natural tendency to seek a religious foundation for his social way of life and that when culture loses its spiritual basis it becomes unstable. Nothing has occurred to alter these facts. Indeed during the last century and a half they have often found a powerful expression in the thought of the age, though not in its social life. Even thinkers who have lost their religious faith, like Comte and Renan and Matthew Arnold, have continued to recognize the sociological necessity of such a relation.

Nor is there any necessary reason why a synthesis should not be possible between a scientific world civilization and a universal and transcendent religion. On the contrary, there is a natural affinity between the scientific ideal of the organization and rationalization of the material world by human intelligence, and the religious ideal of the ordering of human life to a spiritual end by a higher law which has its source in the Divine Reason.

It is almost an historical accident that man's achievement of control over his material environment by science should have coincided with his abandonment of the principle of spiritual order so that man's new powers have been made the servants of economic acquisitiveness and political passion.

The recovery of moral control and the return to spiritual order have now become the indispensable conditions of human survival. But they can be achieved only by a profound change in the spirit of modern civilization. This does not mean a new religion or a new culture but a movement of spiritual reintegration which would restore that vital relation between religion and culture which has existed at every age and on every level of human development.

Index

Abu'l Fazl, 210
African (except Egypt), religion culture, 39, 47, 70, 87, 102, 114, 123–6, 135, 138, 145, 156, 198–9; social organisation, 110, 198–9
Agni, 94, 144
after life, Buddhist beliefs, 184, 186 Egyptian 118; Hindu, 182–3
agriculture, possible religious origin of, 138; *see also* fertility cults
Akbar, 210
Albigensians, 183
Al Ghazali, 33*n*, 77–81
Al Hakim, 126
Al Jilani, Abd al Qadir, 71
Al Muqanna, 82
American Indians (religion culture), 39, 49, 52, 55, 65, 70, 84, 87, 91, 102–3, 134, 136–8, 158–60, 177; Californian, 136–7; Indians of the Plains, 52, 55, 159; Pueblo Indians, 102–3, 158–60; *also* Aztecs, 160; Incas, 114; Maya, 89, 139–40, 160, 197
Amon, 207
Anabaptists, 82
ancestors or culture heroes, divine or semi-divine, 54–6
Anglicanism, 202
animal gods, Egyptian, 116–7; guardians, cult of, 41, 56, 58, 134
Ankole, 198–9
Apaches, 159
Apis bulls, 207
Aratus, 141–2
archaic culture, 88–9, 114–16, 126, 136, 139, 142–3, 145, 156, 158, 162–4, 167, 190, 206–7, 212
Aristotle, 140; quotation from *On Philosophy*, 29–30; from *Metaphysics*, 140–1
Armenians, 203–4
Arnold, Matthew, 105, 217

Arthur, 55
asceticism, 56, 69, 81, 97–9, 134, 177–83, 189, 203
Asha, 146
Asoka, 185
Assassins, 83
astral theology, 140–2
Atman Brahman, identification of, 36, 92, 96, 183
Augustine, St., 77, 90, 91
Aurignacian art, 132
Australian aborigines (religion culture), 51–2, 54–5, 68*n*, 91, 132, 135
Averroes, 79
Avvakum, 205
Azande, 156
Aztecs, 160

Baader, F. von, 11*n*
Babak the Khurammite, 82
Babylonian astral theology, 141; pantheon, 143
Bacon, Francis, 6
Bagyendwana, 199
Bahima monarchies, 114, 198–9
Bairo, 198
Balaam, 70–1
Bantu kingdoms, 198–9
Baur, F. C., 14, 20
Bayle, 9
Benedict, Ruth, 49, 102–3, 134
Benin, 126
Berkeley, Bishop, 8
Bernard de Sahagun, 105
Bernadin de St. Pierre, 12
Berosus, 104
Bhagavad Gita, 188–90, 192
Blake, William, 10–11
Boas, F., 49
Bodhicharyvatara (poem), 187
Bodhisatva, 189
Boehme, Jacob, 11, 12
Bopp, Franz, 15

INDEX

Bracciolini, Poggio, 4
Brahma, 186–7
Brahman, 36, 92, 95–8, 183
Brahmanas, 100–1, 144, 184
Brahmana Satapatha, 95–6
Brahmins, 65, 92–8, 100, 101, 172
Bran, 55
Bridgewater Treatises, 6
Buddha, 98, 163, 184–7; practical deification of, 186–7
Buddhism, 60–1, 98–101, 171–2, 184–90, 192–3, 207, 211; Central Asia, 61, 187; Chinese, 171–2, 187, 189, 192; Kushan Empire, 187; Japanese, 189, 192; Tibet, 60–1, 99; Mahayana, 187–90; Tantric, 99, 193; Zen, 189; influenced by Taoism, 189; unsolved dualism of culture and contemplation, 60, 98–100, 192–3
Bunel, Pierre, 7
Bushmen, 47, 110, 132
Byzantine Empire, religious cultural conflicts within, 209

calendar, 137, 142, 145, 162–3; Mayan, 139–40; Pueblo, 102
California, Indian religion culture, 136–7
Caligula, 126
Calvin, 25–27
Campanella, Tommaso, 5–6
Cartesian philosophy, 7–9; physics, 30
Carvakas, 183*n*
Chadwick, H. M. and N. K., 67–8, 104*n*, 105*n*
China (religion culture), 65, 88, 99–100, 104, 105, 127, 139, 146, 161–72, 176, 181, 189, 192, 197; secularisation, 214
Chou dynasty, 167
Christianity and Hellenism, dualism between, 175–6
Chuang Tzu, 168–9
Chuckchees, 177
Cicero, 26, 29, 141*n*, 206–7
Clarke, Samuel, 155 *and note*
Cleanthes, 141
Comparative Religion, 16–17, 61–2
Comte, Auguste, 17, 106, 217
Congregationalism in New England, 203

contemplative prayer, 189–93; *see also* mysticism
Confucian scholars, 65, 163 *sqq.*, 176, 192
Confucius, 163 *sqq.*, 181
Cook, Captain James, 114
Copernicus, 149
Creuzer, F., 14, 20
culture, definition, 47–8; classification of religion cultures, 57; five or six recent religion cultures, 212; culture and religion, relation between, Chapter VIII *passim*, Chapter X *passim*, 22, 58–9, 98–100, 133, 175 *sqq.*, 208 *sqq.*; culture and contemplation, 98–100, 192–3; cultural changes and religion, Chapter X *passim*; contacts between cultures, 104–5, 114; culture and racial mixture, 160–1, 198 *sqq.*; cultures built pre-eminently by priesthoods, 87–8; mediaeval culture synthesis, 201; western culture identified with civilisation, 213; need of re-integration by religion, 217–8
culture heroes, 54–6
custom, 155–7
cycles of nature, 41; and human life, 137–8, 145, 162–3
Cyrus, 127–8
Czaplicka, M. A., 178

daimonic man, 110–12
Dandoy, Père G., 35*n*, 37
Dante, 149, 201
Dead, Book of the, 121
Deism, 8–10
Delawares, 70
Delphic Oracle, 72
Dervishes, 40, 71, 81
Descartes, 7–9
Dewey, John, 35
Dike, 146
Din Ilahi (Akbar's syncretist religion), 210
Diodorus, 206
Dionysius, cult of, 72
divination, diviners, 66 *sqq.*, 155–7, 163, 167–8; *see also* Shamans, Shamanism
divorce between science and spirit, 20 *sqq.*, 213–18

dreams, 76
dream vision, 52, 57–8, 66, 68–9, 71, 76, 134, 137, 159
Druses, 126n
Dupont de Nemours, P. S., 153

economic explanation of culture, criticism of, 58 sqq.
economics, relation to culture, 131 sqq.
Egypt (religion culture), 50–1, 88, 90, 103, 113–23, 139–40, 143, 197, 206–7; priesthood, 51, 88, 90, 103, 143; divine kingship, 115 sqq.; Nomes, 116; unification of, 116; animal gods, 116–17; after-life beliefs, 118 sqq.; ethics, 120–1; pyramid texts, 118–19; solar cult, 117–23; Iknaton's religious revolution, 122–3
Eloquent Peasant, 121
Emerson, R. W., 105
Empedocles, 43, 147–9, 181
Encyclopaedists, 149
endura, 183
Engels, F., 133
Enlightenment, 6, 9–13, 15, 18, 20, 33, 44, 148–9, 212–13
Enlil, 143
Erasmus, 4
Esquimaux, 47, 110
Ethiopia (religion culture), 123
evolutionary approach to Natural Theology, 16 sqq.
Ezekiel, 127

Fa Hia, 169–71
Faizi, 210
fertility cults, 58, 91, 103, 135, 138–9
fetishism, 39, 102, 135, 199
Ficino, Marsilio, 6
Fifth Monarchy Men, 82, 203–4
Fire Altar, 95
Fox, George, 205
Franciscans, 201
Fraser, Alexander Campbell, 16
Frazer, Sir James George, 133–4
Freeman, Miss K., 72n
Freud, S., 31
Freudian theory of primitive man, 110

Garstang, J., 139
genealogy, interest of primitives in, 113
Germanicus, 141n
Ghazzalian culture, 115
Ghost Dance, 52
Gifford Lectures, 16, 18, 34
Gilgamesh, 115
Gill, W. W., 104, 105n
God of Nature identified with God of the Soul, 35–6, 39
Goethe, 110–11
Greek, see Hellenic
Guillaume, A., 68n

Hahn, E., 138
Halafian culture, 115
Han dynasty, 171
Heaven, Altar of, 162
Hebrew religion, 30, 35, 72–3, 82, 110, 126–8, 154, 200
Hegel, 17
Hellenic religion culture, 36, 43–4, 72, 92–3, 95, 98, 105, 113, 140–2, 145–9, 181, 200; law, 154; philosophy related to religion, 43, 50, 72, 92–3, 95, 98, 147–9
Heracleitus, 72, 147–9
Herodotus, 120
Hesiod, 142
Hinduism, 34–7, 39, 42–3, 92–105, 113, 139–40, 144–9, 177–83, 188–93, 199–204; evolution of sacrifice in, 92 sqq., 144–9, 172; later stages of, 100 sqq.; theistic, 188–9; dualism between culture and contemplation, 192–3; effects of racial mixture, 199; contacts with European religion, 105; see also Brahma, Brahman, Brahmins, Upanishads, Vedas, Vedanta
Hipparchus, 141n
history underlying legend, 55–6
Hocart, A. M., 112
Horus, 115–16, 118
Hugo, Victor, 82
humanism, 4 sqq., 27–8, 37–8, 67, 104–6, 123, 150, 175, 212–14, 216–17
hunters, primitive religion of, 41, 49, 56–8, 91, 115, 133–4, 159

Ibadan, 125

Ibn Khaldun, 74–7
Ifa, 125, 156
Ife, 125–6, 156
Iknaton, 122–3
Incas, 114
Indian religion culture, *see* Buddhism, Hinduism, Jainism *and references there given*
Indo-Iranian art, 100
initiation, 56–7, 134–5, 137–8, 177–8
intichiuma ceremonies, 91
Isaiah, Deutero-, 127–8
Islam, 40, 53, 56, 59, 65, 70–84, 154, 207–8, 211; prophecy in, 65, 70–84; dervishes, 40, 71, 81; religious orders, 71
Ismailians, 83

Jacobi, F. H., 33
Jainism, 98, 183, 204
Jalaluddin Rumi, 71
James, William, 18–20, 30, 32, 40
Japan, religion, 189, 192
Jeremiah, 82
Jericho figurines, 139
Jesuit scholars, 104
Job, Book of, 30, 35
Joubert, J., 12*n*
Jukun, 124
Jung, C. J., 19

Kaivalya, 190
Kanakuk, 70
Kant, 9
Karma, 182, 186
Karma Mimamsa, 101
Kepler, J., 149
Kern, F., 154
Kickapoo, 70
kingship; kings sacred, Chapter VI *passim*, 50, 66, 102, 160, 162–3, 166, 198–9; Bantu, 198–9; Chinese, 127, 162–3, 166; Egyptian, 115–23; Nubian, 123; Old Testament, 126–8; Phoenician, 127; West African, 124–5
kingship of Jahweh opposed in Old Testament to kingship of heathen gods, 126–8
knowledge, sacred, 42–3, 67–8, 88–90, 96–8, 102–6, 135–6, 139–41, 147–50, 179; secularised, 104–6, 149

Krober, A. L., 136–7
Kushan Empire, 187

Lamaism, 60–1, 99
Lammenais, 82
Latourette, K. S., 216
Law of Nature, 7, 153 *sqq.*, 171, 217; Chinese view of, 162 *sqq.*
law, sacred, Chapter VIII *passim*, 208; secularised, 154–5
Law, William, 11*n*
leadership, sacred, 110–12
Leibnitz, 149
Lieh Tzu, 169
Lobeck, C. A., 15
Locke, J., 10
Lono, *see* Cook, Captain James
Lucretius, 38, 84
Lycurgus, 154

Maat, 120
Macdonald, D. B., 77*n*
Machiavelli, 4
Magdalenian art, 132–3
magic, 38–9, 41, 51, 70, 73, 89, 91–3, 95, 99, 103, 121, 133–6, 138, 149, 157, 167, 178
Mahavira, 98
Mahayana, 187–90; *see also* Buddhism
Mahdi, the Sudanese, Mahommed Ahmed, 83
Maistre, Joseph de, 13, 14
Malebranche, N., 8, 149
Mana, 38–9, 113
Manetho, 104
Mangaia, religion of, 104, 105*n*
Manito, 38
Manu, laws of, 13
Maoris, 113
Marduk, 143
Marsilio Ficino, 6
Marxism, 83, 131–3; its economic interpretation of culture criticised, 131–3
Maxim Wledig, 55
Max Müller, F., 15, 16
Maya, 89, 139–40, 160, 197
mediaeval culture synthesis, 201
Meek, C. K., 124
Melanesia, religion culture, 113, 135, 138
Melcarth, 127

Merikere, 120
Mesopotamia, religion culture, 88–90, 100, 103, 114–15; *see also* Babylonian *and* Sumerian
Methodism, 203
Mimamsa, Karma, 101
Mimamsa, Uttara, 44
Mohammed, 59
Mohave, 156–7
moira, 146
moksha, 182, 190
Mongols, 60–1; made peaceful by Buddhism, 61
Monophysites, Syrian, 203
Monotheism, in Buddhism, 187; in Hinduism, 188, 190; tendency to in polytheism, 43, 122–3; *see also* Theism
Montaigne, 6*n*, 7
More, St. Thomas, 4
Mother Goddess, the, 58, 89, 100, 138–9
Muller, K. Ottfried, 15
mystery religions, 135
mysticism, 11–12, 15, 29, 31–5, 37, 39–40, 71, 77–81, 92–3, 96–8, 144, 167–9, 180–1, 189–93; and natural theology, 190 *sqq.*

Napoleon, 111
National Socialism, 83
Natural Law, 153
Natural Theology, follows revealed, 7, 43–4; and mysticism, 190 *sqq.*; psychological approach to, 18–21, 31–4, 37–40
Neo-platonism, 36, 149, 181
Nestorians, Syrian, 203
Newman, Cardinal, 213
Newton, Sir Isaac, 12*n*
Newtonian physics, 30
Nigeria, sacred kingship in, 124–5
Nikon, patriarch, 205
Nirvana, 190, 199, 208
Nonconformity, 202–5
Nubia, subculture in, 123
Numinous, 38–9, 50; as a super-human power in a man, 110–13

Old Believers, 203–5
Oracles, 72, 155–6
Order, Sacred, Chapters VII, VIII and IX, 49–50, 62, 124–6, 204–5; and order of nature, Ch. VII,

especially 137 *sqq*; *also* 124–6; and the social order, Ch. VIII; and the spiritual life, a way of perfection, Ch. IX; cycle of nature and cycle of human life, 137–8, 145, 162–3; relation to law and especially to natural law, 153 *sqq.*, 217; in Chinese culture, 161–72; revolt against, 204–5
Orenda, 38
oriental religions and philosophies discovered by the West, 13 *sqq.*
Orphism, 44, 72, 181
Osiris, 117–18, 121
Otto, Rudolf, 38

Palacios, Miguel Asin, 79
palaeolithic art, 132–3
Palestine, race and religion in, 200
Paley, Archdeacon, 6, 33
Pan-Egyptian theory, 114
Pascal, 8, 20
Paviotso, 55, 70
Peasant, the Eloquent, 121
peasants' culture and warriors', 198, 200; religion of, *see* fertility cults *and* Mother Goddess; *also* 41
Pepi, 118–19
Perry, W. J., 114
Peter the Great, 205
Philosophy, Greek, 43, 50, 72, 92–3, 95, 98, 141–2, 147–9, 181; and astral theology, 141–2; and priest-hood, 92–3, 95, 98; and prophecy, 72, 147–9; religious origin of, 43, 50, 72, 92–3, 95, 98, 147–9
Pigmies, 110
Pindar, 94, 146
Plato, 50, 72*n*, 140, 149
Platonists, Cambridge, 6, 149; Neo-platonists, 36, 149, 181; Renais-sance, 4–5, 67
Poet, relation to religious seer, 66–8; daimonic character of, 110–1
Poggio Bracciolini, 4
Pontiac, 70
Pope, Alexander, 12
Polynesia, religion culture, 38–9, 70, 88, 102, 113–14, 145, 157
Pragnaparamitra Sutra, 193
presence of God in the soul, 32–3
pre-Socratic philosophy, 43, 72, 147–9, 181

priesthood; priests: Ch. V *passim*; 50–1, 65–6, 84, 136–7, 143, 160–2; architects of culture, 87–8; conservatism of, 87; sacrificial aspect of, 90–96, 136; depositories of sacred learning, 87, 89–90, 93 *sqq.*, 103 *sqq.*; and philosophy, 92–3, 95, 98; students of foreign religion cultures, 104–5; secularised, 105; Californian, 137; Christian Europe, 103–4; Egyptian, 51, 88–90; Indian, 65, 92 *sqq.*, 101; Maya, 89; from Near East to China, 88; Pueblo, 102–3, 158; Sumerian 51, 88–90; Zuni, 102–3; synthesis of priestly and warrior cultures, 160–1
Pritchard, E. E. Evans, 156
prophecy, prophets, Chapter IV *passim*, 53–5, 102, 147–9; revolutionary element in, 82 *sqq.*; and philosophy, 72, 147–9; Ibn Khaldun's doctrine of, 74–6; Al Ghazali's, 78–81; American Indian, 52, 55, 69, 70; Hellenic, 72, 147–9; Semitic and in particular Moslem, 70–84; secularist, 82–4
psychological approach to natural theology, 18–21, 31–4, 37–40
Ptah, 143
Ptahhotep, Instruction of, 120
Pueblo Indians, 102–3, 158–60, 136–7, 197
Pwyll, 55
Pyramids, 120
Pyramid texts, 118–19
Pythagoras, Pythagoreans, 43, 147, 149, 181

Quakers, 204–5
Quetzalcoatl, 114

racialism, criticism of, 47–8
racial mixture, its effect on culture, 198–200
Ramanuja, 100, 101n, 190
Rammohun Roy, 105
Ramsay, Sir William Mitchell, 138, 207–8
Raymund Sebunde, 6–7
Re, 117–120
reason, scientific, and the spirit, divorce and possible reconciliation between, 21–2, 44, 216, 218

Reformation, 202
reincarnation, 182–3
religion, conservative and dynamic, 50, 59, 84; and culture, relations between, *see* Culture; five or six religion cultures in modern world, 212; in modern world, 216
religious experience, 79–81. *See also* Mysticism
Renan, 217
Resurrection festival, 138
revelation, authority of, 42–4, 84, 211–12
revolutions, modern, and secularisation, 214
Rita, 144–6
Robespierre, M., 9, 82
romanticism, 10–12
Roman religion, 62, 68n, 84, 157
Rongo, *see* Cook, Captain James
Rousseau, J. J., 9, 82
Ruanda, 198
Ruysbroeck, 32–3

sacrifice, 66, 90, 91, 136, 162, 166, 182; in India, evolution of, 92–8, 101, 136, 144–5, 160, 182
St. Just, A. A. L. de R. de, 82
Samson, 110
Sankara, 42–3, 100, 101n, 190
Santideva, 187
Sanyasis, 40
Schlegel, Friedrich von, 14
Schelling, F. W. J. von, 11, 14–15
science, sacred, *see* knowledge, sacred; and the spirit, *see* reason, scientific, and the spirit
Sebunde, Raymond, 6–7
secret societies, 135, 138
secularisation of society, 4, 27–8, 30–1, 37–8, 49, 82–4, 104–6, 148–9, 154–5, 161, 204–5, 214–18; modern and anomalous, 49; of knowledge, 104–6, 149; of law, 154–5; of priesthood, 104–6; of prophecy, 82–4; ruins culture, 106, 214–18; in later Czarist Russia, 205
Semitic religion, 72 *sqq.*; *see also* Hebrew Religion, Islam
Shamanism, Shamans, 39, 43, 51, 54, 58, 61, 69–70, 75, 89, 135, 177–9
Shamash, 143

INDEX

Shawnees, 70
Shaykhs, 65
Shih Huang Ti (emperor), 170-1
Shradda, 182
Shu, 119
Siberian religion, see Shamanism, Shamans, *especially* 177 *sqq.*
Sieroszcewski, 177-8
sin, sense of, 156-7
Sin (moon god), 143
Sioux, 52
Sivaism, 100
Skinner, A. B., 69
Skoptsy, 203
Smith, G. Elliot, 114
Social conflicts, effect on religion, 209
Socrates, 72n, daemon of, 43
Solon, 154
soma, 93n, 94
Spencer, B., and Gillen, F. J., 51
Spencer, Herbert, 37
Stoics, 141-2, 149
Sumerian religion, 50-1, 88-90, 93, 138-40; priesthood, 51, 88-90
Sunyata, 190
syncretism of gods, 116-17, 142-3, 209; of creeds, 210-11
Syrian religion, heathen, 138
Syrian Nestorians and Monophysites, 203

Taborites, 82
tabu, 157, 198
Tantrism, 99, 193
Tao, 146
Taoism, 167-70, 181, 189, 192; influences Buddhism, 189
Tasmanians, 132
Tecumseh, 70
Tenkswatawa, 70
Tereavai, 105n
Tertullian, 175
theism, proof of from order of the universe, 29-30; from religious experience, 31 *sqq.*; *see also* Monotheism
Thomas Aquinas, St., 79, 191-2
Thoth, 120
Tiaio (shark god), 105n
Tibet (Lamaism), 60-1, 99
Tieck, L., 11n
totemism, 51-2, 54-5, 91, 135-6, 138

Transcendence, Divine, Chapter II *passim, in particular* 29, 32-9; *also* 58, 61, 109, 185, 190-3, 197, 206, 208-9, 211-12; cosmological and psychological, 31-2, 35-6, 39
transmigration of souls, 182-3
Tsin Empire, 169-71
Tylor, J. B., 16, 47

Uganda, 110, 198-9
Ulema, 84
Unyoro, 198
Upanishads, 44, 94, 96-8, 144, 148, 179-84, 190; Maitrayana Upanishad, 179-81; Mundaka Upanishad, 97

Vanaprasthas, 179
Vanini, Lucilio, 4
Varuna, 144-5
Veda, Atharva, 93n, 97; Rig, 93-4, 97, 144-5, 148, 182; Sama, 93n, 97; Yajur, 93n, 97
Vedanta, 35-7, 39, 42-4, 94, 96-8, 100-1, 144, 148, 179-84, 190
Vedas, 95-7, authority of, 42-3
Vegetation god, 138-9
Vidyarsagar, Iswar Chandra, 105
Vishnuism, 100
Voltaire, 9

Wakan, 38
Wakonda, 69
warrior cultures, 159-61, 198, 200; and peasant, 198, 200; and theocratic, 160-1
Wells, H. G., 215
Williams, Roger, 204
Wolff, Christian, 10
Wovoka, 52, 55, 70

Xenophanes, 149

Yakut, 177-8
Yoga, Yogis, 40, 183, 188
Yok, 38
Yoruba, 125, 156
Yuma, 136-7
Yves de Paris, 6

Zarathustra, 163
Zeno, 141n
Zeus, 141-2
Zuni, 102-3